How to
Be Happy
When You're Single

And You Don't
Want to Be Single

One-derful Life

Heart-to-Heart Chats That Make Sense

Mary R. Dittman

How to Be Happy When You're Single (And You
Don't Want to Be Single)

ISBN: 978-0-578-53984-3

To My Bunny, Hannah Mae

Table of Contents

Introduction to The One-Derful Life

Even though I've had a wildly successful
career as a teacher, writer, speaker, and
marketing expert, my singleness has always been
a deep source of sadness for me.

While I love my career, I've always wanted to
be married and have a family. True, my 20's were
focused on building my career. I wanted a
relationship in my 30's, but even though they
never seemed to work out, I had hope because I
figured I still had plenty of time.

By the time my 40's rolled around, I realized I
needed to make peace with being single. I was
deeply unhappy in my singleness. I dreaded
every holiday, birthday, and the inevitable
engagement announcements of all of my friends.

I searched every book, program, and
philosophy for help. There was a lot of
information out there on how to find a man, how
to be happy until a man comes along, and how to
come to the realization that you DON'T need a
man. But there didn't seem to be anything to
help me.

My problem was that I didn't want to be
single, but I was, and I didn't know if that would
ever change, but I just wanted to be happy
anyway.

That's what launched One-Derful Life. I was
cobbling together advice and help - most of it not

geared towards singleness - and adapting it to fit my situation.

To me, a One-Derful Life is one where I have made peace with being single. I don't prefer it! I would prefer marriage and family. But, I just want to be happy. And not that fake happy where you smile and tell people you're content, but you're really depressed and bitter (done that).

A One-Derful Life means you're content and at peace. You're creating a life you love. This is the energy that will attract your Mr. Right (men love happy women!). But even if he never shows up, you'll be happy. And, isn't that what you really want, anyway?

I started writing for a local women's magazine, and my column became one of the most popular and widely read. Even though it was geared to single women over 35, it was read by men, married women, and ladies of all ages.

Since then, One-Derful Life has become a blog, a weekly TV show on Facebook and YouTube, a podcast (hosted on SoundCloud), and now a book. With more to come, I hope!

This book is a collection of my earliest writings. You can read it cover-to-cover, but each chapter stands alone. This way, if you're struggling with something or only want to read about a particular subject, you can just read the short chapter to get what you need.

Thank you for picking up this book. I hope it will help you on your own journey of singleness and assist you in creating your own One-Derful Life.

You can always connect with us at One-DerfulLife.com. We post a new blog there every Friday, and we have some cute One-Derful Life merchandise you should check out!

Okay, let's get started!

Worse than Being 40 and Single

Remember that line from the movie *When Harry Met Sally*? Sally is crying over her ex-boyfriend's impending marriage when she wails, "But I'm gonna be 40!"

That was funny to me in my 20's when that movie came out, but when I was turning 40, it wasn't so humorous.

I moved to a small Southern town when I was 24 years old and focused on my career.

To be honest, I was never very interested in marriage or having a family until I turned 30.

By then, however, I was dating the wrong men – guys who told me they didn't want a commitment, guys that I would not have been compatible with, guys that were still in love with other girls.

When I did meet a nice man, I was so focused on getting him to the altar that I would invariably run him off with my intensity and desperation.

This desperation was compounded by the fact that I live in a small, Southern town where most people are married with children and there is not really a defined singles community.

It always intrigues me that when I visit people in cities like Las Vegas, San Francisco, Los Angeles, and New York, nobody asks me if I'm married or if I have children. They're just interested in getting to know ME.

In my town, however, I frequently am asked to explain WHY I'm single; people even go so far as to ask me what's wrong with me.

Additionally, our national culture is very focused on being part of a couple.

The diet, health, fashion, and beauty industries exist to sell us products to help us attract someone.

Then there are lines from movies that set us up for emotional disaster: "You complete me."

The message is, you can't be happy unless you have found your soul mate.

I was truly enslaved for most of my 30's by this quest to "find someone."

I've done it all: online dating, joining civic groups to "get out there," long distance relationships, church singles groups, etc.

It seemed like the more I did to try to find someone, the lonelier I felt.

All of my friends got married – I threw bridal showers and stood up at their weddings, I organized engagement parties and plastered a "happy for you" smile on my face.

Eventually, I threw baby showers, and attended first birthday parties – usually without a date – and always having to explain why I was still single.

I felt like all my peers had passed me by and I was stuck in some adolescent nightmare where "family holiday" still referred to my parents, not my own family.

Don't get me wrong – I could have been married 10 times by now. But have you ever noticed the ones that want to marry you aren't the ones you want to marry?

When I was in my mid-thirties, I realized that I needed to make some decisions about my life.

If I wanted to have children, I needed to get married and have them, get pregnant, or look into adopting.

A lot of my single friends struggle with this issue; I admit, I am lucky that I really never was that excited about having children alone.

One of my friends told me that, "People who don't want children are mentally ill," but I disagree. I think some women just don't have a strong maternal instinct. Either way, I realized that I wasn't that upset about not having children.

So, if I didn't want children, I had to ask myself why I was in such a hurry to get married.

The reason: I felt like I was single because there was something wrong with me. I felt nobody had "picked" me because of some defect in me.

I know I'm not alone in feeling like that because I have talked to countless women – and men – who have felt that way in singleness.

I was convinced that if I could only get married, I would be happy.

Everything else in my life was great – wonderful, fulfilling career, I owned my own home, my finances were in order, I was providing for my retirement, I have great friends, I'm healthy.

But that one missing piece: no one to "complete me." Therefore, I felt worthless – a feeling that is made worse when you live in a small town where people's primary focus is getting married and having children.

And it gets much worse (in my experience) after age 35 because the worthlessness is compounded by a feeling of hopelessness.

But I know a lot of really great single men and women and I never look at them and think, "wow, you're actually a failure and a loser because you're single."

And most of my friends report that they don't think less of me for being single. So what's the deal?

My BFF says you have to be happy first. That's the conventional wisdom. Be happy and you'll attract the "right person."

I had to face the fact that at my age, living in a small town, I may never meet "the right person." That is a scary thought, but once I came to accept that maybe this was it – just me making a life for myself, I realized it's not so bad. In fact, it's pretty good!

I can do what I want, go where I want, spend what I want, date whom I want. Especially when I stopped romanticizing marriage as a cure-all.

Ask your married friends about the down sides of marriage. If marriage is the key to happiness, why is the divorce rate nearly 50% on first marriages? Not being negative, but be realistic: no one thing can cure your unhappiness. Not the right job, not the right car, not the right weight, not the right person.

I started to focus on having a great life – whether or not my last name ever changed. And 90% of the time, I really love my life.

I do wish I could find that "special someone," but it's also great to be able to walk away from someone who is not so special.

I think we all know that there are worse things than "being alone."

Talk to someone who is in a bad marriage. Talk to someone who is isolated and lonely but can't go meet Prince Charming because they're already married to Prince Jerky.

Hang in there, single friends. There's something worse than being single and 40. It's being single, 40, and having an unfulfilled life because you've been waiting for someone to come save you from yourself.

There's nothing wrong with you, so get out there and start living that One-Derful Life.

Bloom Where You're Planted: A Single Flower Gets All the Attention!

The Apostle Paul said he had "learned the secret to being content." I'm not sure what Paul's secret was, but I believe one secret to being content in your singleness is to "bloom where you're planted."

I used to be confused by Jesus' parable of the talents.

In this parable, several servants are given talents (money) and then judged based on what they did with them. The servant who didn't earn at least a minimal return on his talents was punished, and his talents were given to the more successful servant. I wonder if this parable is telling us to do the most we can with what we are given.

My best friend used to tell me I had to be happy being single before I could be happy being married.

But I had a lot of years where I felt like I could NOT be happy being single because I only wanted to be married.

Sort of a Catch 22 – need to be happy alone, but can't be happy if I'm alone. What to do?

To me, "bloom where you're planted" means "take care of what you currently have."

I remember that when I was a little girl, I wanted a new Barbie doll. But I had cut all the hair off my other Barbies and played with them outside and generally not taken good care of them. My parents told me I wouldn't be getting any new Barbies until I proved to them that I could take care of my toys.

If that's how earthly parents handle their children, it makes sense to me that our Heavenly Father won't entrust us with more and more if we're not taking care of what we have now.

Think about it like this: how do you get a promotion at work? You do an excellent job, show up early, stay late, take on extra tasks, have a positive attitude, support others, treat the customers right, respect your boss, and do your best.

Now, that doesn't guarantee you'll get a promotion, but if you don't do those things, you can be sure you WON'T get a promotion!

Well, the same is true in life. If you show up fully in your current life, treat people lovingly, respect the Boss, do your best, you're more likely to be given more.

But first you have to show that you can take care of your little corner of the garden.

Here is the secret to my personal contentment regarding the single life: I decided to show up fully in my current life.

That meant treating my relationships (casual dates, friends, family) with love and respect, serving others (hey, I don't have a family to cook dinner for, so I can cook meals for people who are sick or bereaved), taking care of my single friends, keeping my home tidy, doing volunteer work that I enjoy, participating in Bible study, and just enjoying the life I currently have.

It seems to me that many singles think they will be happier if they are married (or coupled), but ask anyone who is part of a couple, and they will tell you that while a good relationship is a blessing, even the best marriage brings some additional challenges.

At the very least, you have to give up some things for a successful relationship. You're not going to get your way all the time.

Nobody has a perfect life. Even the 3 people you're envious of probably don't have it all that great.

If you were able to look behind closed doors, you would find something that isn't so great.

A lot of your married friends are envious of your freedom and time to yourself and free time, I can promise you.

I don't believe God makes people be single if they don't want to be, but I do believe He will use anything and everything for His plan – He can use us to bless others IF WE LET HIM.

You have a choice: you can choose to be bitter in your singleness, or you can choose to be BETTER in your singleness.

You can choose to be happy or you can choose to be negative. The choice is yours. If you have decided you cannot be happy unless you have your way, God isn't going to reward your attitude.

Again, think about your work life. Does your boss give you a raise and a promotion when you pout, stomp around, and complain about things not going the way YOU wanted them to go?

In the spirit of blooming where you are planted, let me share with you some of the benefits I have experienced in my single life that my married friends are jealous of: I can dump a guy if he's irritating me. I can go to the symphony, theatre, all the movies I like, sporting events, and church without anyone complaining or feeling left behind.

I can have dinner with my girlfriends and not get into an argument about it. I can decorate the rooms in my house any color I like. I can spend as much money as I want on shoes and handbags.

I can lie around in my fuzzy pink bathrobe. I have time to read. I can travel anywhere I like. I can watch whatever I want to on TV. I can cook what I want to eat, or eat frozen entrees every night of the week.

I challenge you to make your own list of things that are good about being single. That doesn't mean you'll be single forever, but it will help you be grateful for where you currently are.

You never know how your life is going to help others, so bloom where you're planted and show God and others that you can be a mature adult and you can learn the secret of contentedness.

Remember: a happy, confident woman is attractive. So, learn to be content, confident, and happy by blooming to your full beauty where you're currently planted.

Getting Un-Stuck

I had conversations with two different girlfriends over the holidays one year – both with the same theme: longing for change. The common theme in both talks was that my friends are feeling "stuck."

One friend is fairly content: she is happy with her job, in a good relationship, and satisfied with the way her life is going. She shared with me that she is feeling "bored," and would like something new to challenge her.

My other friend is in a less contented place: she is unfulfilled in her job, and she works from home so she isn't able to socialize as much. Additionally, she owns a house with her parents, and is not happy with her home life (which is also her work environment). She told me she needs to do something different because she is "so miserable" in her life.

Maybe you can relate to one of my friends? Perhaps you feel bored with the comfortable routine of your life; or, maybe you are closer to the "miserable" end of the continuum.

Feeling "stuck" in a rut can be anything from a little ditch to a gaping hole.

The good news is, you can do something new anytime.

You may have some goals – losing weight, decluttering your house, saving money – but what if you long for something more, something deeper?

You might be content with your life, but still feel like something is missing – a little empty space in your soul that you can't quite put your finger on. Do you long for adventure or challenge?

We can't always control the circumstances of our lives, but we can control how we are operating within those circumstances.

You may not feel like you can quit your job – you have responsibilities, you have your retirement, or you're content with your work.

Even if you long for a new challenge, there may not be an opportunity for a promotion or for a transfer.

However, maybe you could work to develop some new skills.

When I was on the product management team at a production facility, I recognized that I didn't know very much about how our products were manufactured. I secured permission from my boss to spend four hours every day with various departments in the factory – as long as I completed my assigned tasks on time and completely.

This self-assigned education in production was very challenging and intimidating, but very valuable.

When you look at your skills, is there something you're missing? Do you know how to use the latest technology tools in your industry? Do you read literature related to your work? Do you need to get some additional training?

Some ideas: training on using social media to increase your business; graphic design courses; continuing education that is outside of your "comfort zone."

Maybe you could take some Spanish classes in order to communicate with the growing Latinx population.

Here's another question: does your workspace (office, cubicle, classroom) show others that you are a valuable, efficient professional? Does your space set a good example to others and inspire you to do your best? Do you need to upgrade your filing system, get rid of the knick-knacks, or cull through the stacks of paper and clutter?

Can you start a new initiative at work? That's easy for me as a teacher: I can build new ideas into my curriculum or work with students or colleagues to begin a new organization on campus. Could you start a book club at work? How about a walking group? A competitive intelligence program?

Of course, you may find your "new" outside the office! How about reading more (and I don't mean more Twitter posts or Pinterest pins)?

Take a class - check out local colleges and universities, adult education programs, and a host of online institutions that offer endless options: photography, sculpture, languages, literature, history, business, fitness, welding, science, philosophy, engineering.

Try growing something: herbs, tomatoes, philodendrons.

Try some new recipes.

Pick up a once-loved hobby. I am renovating a dollhouse that my dad and I built when I was a little girl. My hope is to give it to my niece in a few years. I'm having fun remodeling, painting, and dreaming about the miniature upgrades I can make.

You may have to try a few different things before you find the one (or more) that helps you uncover your One-Derful Life.

Don't give up! Be willing to try a variety of activities – that alone could be the new challenge you long for.

How to Heal a Broken Heart

I have a lot of experience with heartbreak, so I am well-qualified to help you heal those wounds and move forward. And you want to move forward so that you can have a One-Derful Life.

Time. You cannot bypass the healing process if you want to truly move past heartache. There are plenty of theories about the amount of time it "should" take to get over something, but the truth is, it depends on you, your emotional investment, your support system, and your commitment to getting over it.

Make a clean break. You cannot get over a wound if you keep injuring yourself.

Think about it: a cut won't heal if you keep digging at it. Likewise, you're not going to get over your heartbreak if you keep hanging around the person who broke it.

This is why dating people you work with can be perilous – you can't get away from seeing them every day!

Throw out the reminders, or pack them away where you can't see them. Stop calling, texting, social media stalking, asking friends about them, or socializing with them.

Mourn your loss. You may try to tell yourself you don't care, and if you don't, you don't have a broken heart!

Your friends will bright-side you and tell you how lucky you are to have gotten out of the relationship when you did; they love you and

21

want you to get back to happy as soon as possible.

However, you need to give yourself space to acknowledge and honor your feelings. It's better if you don't torpedo your career by crying in your office or calling out sick for a week, but if you absolutely need a day to lie around and grieve, take a mental health day.

As you move through the process, allot yourself a specific amount of time - one hour, one afternoon, 10 minutes – to cry and wallow.

Talk it out. I'm a huge proponent of talk therapy. I started seeing a therapist when I had one doozy of a heartache, and she helped me through a lot of life's valleys.

Come to think of it, that's proof that I CAN commit: I was with one therapist for 15 years.

Therapy is great because you don't run the risk of burning out your friends and family with your constant rehashing of events and questions as to why things fell apart.

A therapist also gives you a safe environment to voice your feelings, as opposed to an unsafe environment: your workplace, social media, the side of your ex's car.

Be honest. It's important to be honest, at least with yourself, about the hurt, disappointment, anger, and other emotions you are feeling. You don't need to express them to others, but you do need to give a voice to them within your own soul.

Strive to accept reality. Whether you ended the relationship or your beloved ended it, it's over. You are going to have to accept this and move on.

Living in the past and mentally rehashing what could have been will only keep you stuck in your pain.

You are not that relationship. Just because your relationship failed, you are not a failure.

Most relationships don't last forever, so having a relationship fail puts you in the "norm" with the majority of people. Try not to categorize your entire life on one relationship or even a series of relationships.

You will not always hurt this badly. Trust me: the pain goes away. Don't create more problems for yourself by acting out of your heartache.

If you focus on moving forward, you can look forward to your heart healing. It does take time, but you can believe that one year from now (or sooner!) you will not be feeling the way you feel now.

Some of the most painful breakups I've experienced have helped me define what I do and do not want in my relationships. In that sense, the breakup served a valuable purpose because now I can avoid some of the painful situations I've encountered.

For today, instead of focusing on what you DON'T have, focus on what you do have: a One-Derful chance to heal and move forward into the good things that are ahead.

I Want to Change (Or Do I?)

"People think that the way you make a change is that you wait for it to feel natural or easy. But transformation comes from being willing to be uncomfortable or uncertain. You have to dive right into not knowing. It's hard at first, but the process gets easier over time." (Kelly McGonigal, Ph.D., *Yoga Journal*, October 2012, p. 96.)

I don't like change. Change is hard. Change is scary. Change means things won't be the same (obviously), and I won't know what to do. Don't we all think this sometimes?

At the heart of our dislike for change is the fear that if things change, *I won't be okay.* Even if things aren't so great right now, at least I know what I'm dealing with.

I believe that at some points in our lives, God does for us what we are unable (or unwilling) to do for ourselves.

I had been needing to make some changes in my life for quite some time: cease certain destructive behaviors, end toxic relationships, and step out in some new directions. Needing to change and actually changing are not the same, however.

Then, I started having panic attacks. Severe panic attacks. I was in my early 40's, and I had never been to an urgent care facility. In fact, I hadn't set foot in an emergency room for my own treatment since I left home at 19.

However, when my third severe panic attack had me convinced I was probably having a heart attack (if not a stroke), I took myself to an urgent care facility while vacationing.

After a quick trip home and a thorough exam the next day, my doctor pronounced me free from heart disease. We determined I was suffering from extreme anxiety due to some other body chemistry issues; anxiety that was sure to subside as my body regulated itself.

While my panic attacks were not triggered by any specific behaviors or situations, I felt it was necessary for me to make some important changes to try to minimize the anxiety. While I might not prevent anxiety with these changes, at least I wouldn't exacerbate it, I figured.

One of the changes I made was dietary. I'm not proud of this, but (like many women – and men!) I am an emotional eater. (The only reason I am willing to write about this is because when I have mentioned this to people, most of them look at me knowingly as they admit to doing the same thing!)

I didn't overeat every day; not even every week. But enough that it was a problem for me. I could go 2 or 3 weeks "being good," but then I would "reward" myself with a ridiculous amount of sugar (that's my food drug of choice).

Of course, then I would have the food hangover for 2 or 3 days, followed by punishing myself by "being extra good" and working out harder to "pay for" what I'd eaten.

I cannot directly link bingeing on sugar with my panic attacks, but I do believe there is a relationship between the two. So, I stopped overeating, and I started really limiting my sugar intake. That was hard for me, because food is my entertainment, my escape, and my reward. I don't drink, I don't use any drugs, but I like cookies (I like a lot of cookies, actually). I enjoy polishing off an entire package of cupcakes in one sitting.

I had to change my thinking about my "comfort food," realizing it's harming my body, not comforting me. There is nothing beneficial for my body in junky sweets. And it is harmful to me when I eat them until I am nauseous. Not to mention the mental damage that follows as I punish myself for my eating.

I also dug more deeply into my yoga practice. I started doing yoga in college to help relieve sciatic nerve pain, and I have practiced yoga on and off since that time. Mostly off, but now, I am very much "on."

Sometimes I feel resentful in yoga class. Usually resentment aimed at the teacher who is leading us into postures that are difficult for me. I don't like some of those yoga poses! They are uncomfortable, I feel like a failure, and I become angry with my own body.

However, by breathing through those postures, by allowing my body to do whatever it can do on that particular day, and by "staying on my own mat" (a yogi phrase for minding your own business and not comparing yourself to and competing with others), I have learned how to be okay with where I am today.

I have also learned that I can do some things that I didn't know I could do. Recently in a yoga class, the teacher demonstrated a series of postures we would be doing, and my immediate thought was, "I can't do that." As if reading my mind, the teacher instructed us to "just try."

I was shocked to see that I actually was able to complete the postures as instructed. I was so excited over my progress! And, that gave me the courage to try advancing a few more postures.

I am happy to report that my panic attacks have subsided. I have bouts of lingering anxiety, but I am learning to manage it (without packaged desserts).

I didn't "feel like" making these changes, but the difficult transitions have led to true transformation in my life, and that transformation has resulted in a greater sense of peace, a stronger connection to God, and more confidence in my own ability to navigate this existence.

So, bring on the change. It's pretty One-Derful.

Is It Love or Fear?

A Course in Miracles proposes that there are only two emotions: love and fear.

At first blush, that's difficult to agree with. What about anger? What about envy? What about grief? When you dig deeper, however, you can link every emotion back to a root of love or fear.

I get angry when things don't go the way I want them to go. Some people say that's because I'm a "control freak." That may be partially true, but WHY do I need to control situations and outcomes?

Because I'm AFRAID I won't be alright if I don't know what's going to happen. I don't trust in God, the Universe, myself, or in the general concept that things will work together for my good.

Why are we envious? We want what other people have and we're AFRAID we won't be happy if we don't get them.

Or, we're AFRAID we're inferior if we don't have that possession or experience that others have.

Grief. Maybe a lot of our grief is fear – fear that we have lost a person or situation that we think we need to survive. Fear that we won't be able to go on. Fear that we'll never be happy again.

Sometimes we have fear because of circumstances related to our grief: health concerns, financial problems, loneliness.

If you've lost anything (we all have) – a relationship, a job, a dream, a loved one - you have experienced grief.

But even in your darkest moments, you can find yourself smiling over a memory. Sometimes you can close your eyes and remember the happy times and the love you felt. I wonder if we grieve because we are AFRAID of change.

When I honestly evaluate my love status, I frequently find that I tend to be very fear-driven. I really don't like that about myself. I'm getting better, but it's still a struggle to focus on love – the positive.

Recently, my pastor challenged the congregation to identify idols we may have in our lives.

I have some pretty typical modern-day idols: I want my way, I want various material possessions, I focus on the material rather than the spiritual. And then it hit me: my commitment to fear is an idol.

No matter what you believe spiritually, you can probably agree that there are two sides to the Universe: positive (love) and negative (fear).

Even if you think you're neutral on something, I suggest that you're not negative, so you're at least leaning toward the positive. So, are you committed to the positive or to the negative in life?

It makes me sad to admit that I struggle with being committed to the negative. I used to think of myself as "realistic" – being prepared for the "worst case scenario." But then I realized I rarely expect the best case.

Don't get me wrong – it's important and wise to see life realistically, and it is a good idea to be prepared for various outcomes.

Let me share an example: recently a friend and I were talking about our health. My friend's mother had breast cancer (and thankfully, she survived and has been cancer-free for more than 20 years), and my friend said, "I'm going to have breast cancer, too." YIKES!

And that's not the first time she's said that! I know the statistics. Yes, if an immediate member of your family has or has had breast cancer, that does increase your risk. Yes, you need to take precautions – get regular checkups and mammograms, do self examinations, do everything you can to be healthy.

But don't just give up and start claiming you're going to have cancer! Don't curse your own life.

Perhaps some of you have the mindset that "if you don't expect good things, you won't be disappointed when you don't get them."

I struggle with that one, too. The problem is, if you never expect good things, you probably won't ever get them.

Another example: sometimes when I have to confront a company where I'm the customer, I brace myself for battle. I go in, ready to argue for the refund I want, prepared to demand to see a manager, and expecting to leave seething with anger.

My best friend, however, expects good service and to be treated well. And she usually is. Because she's nice – she's not uptight with her dukes up, ready for a throw down. The old "self-fulfilling prophecy."

I heard it this way once: "believers are supposed to BELIEVE." You have put your faith somewhere.

Where's your faith? If you're believing in the good, you're in a healthy state of love.

If you're constantly waiting to be hit on the head by the proverbial anvil falling out of the sky, you're in a full-on state of fear.

Here's one way to test your love versus fear ratio: how often do you say things like: "Well, what's going to go wrong next?" Or, "Things never work out for me." Or, "It's just one (bad) thing after another."

We seem to believe that being negative and fearful and expecting to suffer is somehow the spiritual path. Like God is somehow blessed and glorified when we're fearful and suffering.

But what's the point of being a Believer if we're going to believe in fear and suffering? And who would want to join us?

Which isn't to say that things will always go the way we'd like them to – folks, that's life on life's terms.

But what if we could start to believe that God (the Universe, Creation, Fate – call it what you will) LOVES us enough to be able to help us to not only survive the difficult times, but also to thrive.

For the next 7 days, I challenge you to put your finger on the pulse of your love. Are you choosing love or fear?

If it's fear, exercise your ability to MAKE A DIFFERENT CHOICE.

But only if you want a One-Derful Life.

Non-Mother's Day

It's Mother's Day. And, once again, you may feel left out if you're not a mom.

Maybe you're like me, and you really don't want to have children (but you'd love to be a stepmom!). Or, perhaps you do want children, but you don't have them now.

In the same way that there is an upside to being single, there is an upside to not being a mother.

Now, I know this is a very painful subject for many women. Maybe you are struggling with the loss of a child, infertility, or having to let go of the dream of having a family.

I would never try to "bright side" you about those situations. However, on a day when you are open to it, you can read this.

For the rest of you – here are some of the benefits of not being a mom. Maybe you will have children someday, or maybe you won't, and you're at peace with that. Either way, you don't want to be miserable every day, so you may as well enjoy this time without "little ones."

You can sleep. Ask any of your friends (or even complete strangers), and they will tell you that when you have kids, you also have a nasty case of sleep deprivation.

The kids aren't tired. They wake up in the middle of the night. They're sick. They're teenagers and out past curfew, so you're up because you vacillate between anger ("they

33

better be home soon!") and worry ("what if they're in a ditch?").

Forget sleeping late on the weekends – the kiddos are up at 5 a.m. ready for playtime and breakfast.

Think you're going to ignore the noise and sleep anyway? Hope you have some good cleaning supplies to fix the damage wrought upon your personal property by unsupervised tots!

You have more money. Children are expensive. Period.

You have freedom. Now that my best friend has 2 children, she isn't available to go out and shop, see a movie, or go to dinner.

If it's whatever sports season it is for children, she spends 5 nights a week at either practice or games. Yawn.

When she was married with no kids, she could tell her hubby it was "girls night out" and leave him a casserole to heat up.

These days, if there's not a kids' event on the calendar, she has to ask if her husband minds babysitting so she can go to dinner or a movie or the mall.

You can take a shower. Ask a woman with a child under the age of 2 how hard it is to get away and take a shower. Let alone get dressed, put on makeup, dry your hair, or straighten up the house.

One of my girlfriends gave up going to the discount store because the process of dressing herself and the children; loading up the stroller, snacks, diaper bag, and remembering her pocketbook were all too exhausting.

Then there was navigating through a public place with 2 children who are enchanted with every piece of merchandise on a shelf, paying for said merchandise, loading it into the car, and then unloading it and putting it away while trying to pacify two children who are now cranky because the excursion wore them out.

You can own nice things. One thing I really do love about not having children is that my sets of everyday crystal, flatware, and heirloom china are all still intact.

I'm not saying a tumbler is more important than a child, but I like the fact that I can have some nice possessions.

There has never been a grilled cheese sandwich in my DVD player, either. My lipstick has never been used to color the walls in my house. My car is neat and clean (my BFF's car totally freaks me out – there is probably a week's worth of discarded snacks, trash, and maybe an as-yet-undiscovered life form growing in her vehicle).

I wonder if her kids are "always sick" not because of day care, but from contracting an exotic disease in the family car.

You do not have to buy 10 boxes of Girl Scout cookies to support your daughter's Scout troop. Okay – maybe the moms win on this one – they can buy 10 boxes of Thin Mints "to support my daughter's Scout troop," where my 10 boxes (a) were just a bad decision (because) (b) they ended up on my tush and thighs. (Which was fantastic for my personal trainer – I purchased another 12 sessions after Cookiegate. However, I do hope I know a Girl Scout next year because I already know I'm going to do it all again. Please call me.)

The probability that someone pee-pees, poo-poos, or throws up on you is pretty low (unless you're hanging out in some questionable local establishments, but I'm not here to judge). And, nobody will hand you his or her nose goblins to dispose of.

I know Mother's Day can be tough if you are longing for a family. Even if you're not, it's easy to feel left out.

But there are pros and cons to every situation. Sometimes I am jealous of my friends who have families; some have confided to me that they are jealous of me.

One of my friends recently confessed to feeling trapped in a loveless marriage where she is basically a single parent. She is exhausted, lonely, and fed up.

At least when I feel that way, I can take a bubble bath or go on a vacation. She can't leave.

If your dream is to one day have children, I hope it comes true and that you will receive the desire of your heart. In the meantime, though, try to enjoy this season. Once you have children, you can never get back to where you are now.

Because even when the kids are grown and gone, you're still their mom and you still worry, and you still cry for them, and you may still have to send them money.

So go shopping, take a nap, and enjoy some peace and quiet - it's a One-Derful Life!

Spiritual Goals

I'm a spiritual woman. I love God. I'm a
Christian. Yet, when I'm setting my goals, I tend
to skip over "the spiritual."

Until my pastor preached a sermon on our
spiritual goals. Honestly, I had never considered
goals in my spiritual life.

I mean, I'm not interested in reading the Bible
through in a year. Plus, how do you set a goal on
God? To me, spiritual goals seemed like a way of
trying God to see if He'll jump through my hoops
and do what I want.

But as I thought about spiritual goals more in-
depth, I realized I have goals for many
relationships in my life (spend more time with
this friend; reach out to that family member; call
the folks I don't see regularly).

Those goals are never about what I want the
other person to do, they're about what I want to
do to better the relationship.

Most motivation experts will say you want to
set goals that are tied to YOUR behavior because
that is all you have control over.

I mentioned reading the Bible through in a
year: some people really enjoy that, and I think
it's great but it's just not a goal that resonates
with me.

I struggle with religious legalism, and I would
be tempted to read my "required quota" so I
could check it off my list, but I wouldn't be
reading out of desire or pleasure, I would be
reading to say I did it.

For my spiritual goals, I imagined what I would like my relationship with God to be like.

I want to trust God and grow in my faith, believing He has a good plan for my life that is so much better than anything I could imagine or hope for.

I want to remember to pray first (instead of panicking or posting on social media), and I want to enjoy my relationship with God.

I want my spiritual life to be something that energizes me and gives me hope, not something that makes me judgmental and rigid.

From there, I learned that if I want to grow in my faith, I have to actively choose to trust the Lord.

By the way – that means He's going to send me situations where I have to rely on Him rather than myself or others.

I have to spend time with God every day. I have to set aside time every day – even just 5 minutes – to pray in a focused and intentional way.

I also have to be available to listen, which means sitting quietly (meditation) or having peace in my spirit so I can hear the "still, small voice" of the Holy Spirit.

If you have a health goal, you need to do something EVERY DAY to get you closer to your goal. That's true in any area of life, and it's true in your spiritual life.

You have to do something every day to intentionally be closer to God. He promises throughout His word that we will find Him when we seek him. And WE have to seek Him – we can't grow our relationship with God through someone else.

We have to invest time in getting to know Him. God is no respecter of persons (see Acts 10:34), so we can be encouraged when God blesses other people.

Don't be jealous and discouraged, take heart knowing that what God does for one, He'll do for you (if you're being faithful – make sure you're being obedient like maybe your friend was!).

God has a One-Derful plan for each of us and the best way to discern that plan is with an individual relationship with Him.

Top 5 Mistakes Singles Make

When I was in my 30's, I thought the worst thing that could happen to me would be to turn 40 and still be single.

Well, I'm years past 40, still single, and have actually reached a place where I'm happy and content - even though I would prefer NOT to be single.

Over the years, I have made many mistakes in my singleness, and there are some bits of advice I'd like to go back give to 30-year old Mary.

Here are the Top 5 Mistakes Singles Make (that are making your life harder!):

One: Thinking a relationship will solve every problem.

I used to think, "If I only had someone," life would be better. I wouldn't feel lonely, I'd feel like my life had purpose, I'd feel loved and valued.

However, most of the women I know who are currently in relationships DO NOT feel loved or valued.

Many times, they do feel lonely, or they crave some space to be alone, if only for a few minutes!

The truth is, a bad relationship brings more problems, and even the best relationship brings different problems.

Your beloved may not be able to help you out financially, may not be able to fix anything around your house, and most assuredly will not be able to "rescue" you from your everyday life.

Two: Worrying about the future.

I wasted a lot of time worrying if I'd be okay if I ended up single.

I said to a friend once, "I hope I'll be okay if I end up single."

To which she replied, "You're single now and you ARE okay." That was really a light bulb moment for me.

My "okay-ness" wasn't in the future – I am alright (more than alright!) right now. Yes, I would prefer to be in a relationship, but I don't need to worry about being alright – I'm already making it as a single person. Hint: you are, too!

Three: Thinking life will be easier with a partner.

Most of my married and coupled friends have shared with me that a relationship brings its own challenges – if you've ever dated anyone for a period of time, you know this is true.

One of my friends moved in with his girlfriend, and 6 weeks later she went through a major health crisis and needed him to take care of her. Not the carefree cohabitation he was dreaming of!

Some things may be easier with a partner – if you like the same things.

If I'm dating someone who likes the symphony and wants to go with me, that's great.

But I've dated men who don't like that sort of thing and when I go alone they pout and blow up my phone during the concert so that I can't enjoy my evening of beautiful music!

A lot of things are easier when you're single. You can spend your money however you want;

you can decorate your home however you like; you can go where you want to go and spend time with whomever you choose.

Four: Waiting to do things.

When I was in college, I mentioned to the guy I was dating that my favorite opera of all time (La Boheme) was being performed live in our town.

I waited for him to ask me out for an evening at the opera – which he did, about two weeks after the show ended.

I vowed then to never again miss an event because I didn't have a date.

If you want to go to something, go. If you want to buy a house, buy one. If you want to travel, do it. Don't wait – what if your soulmate never shows up? Don't miss out on YOUR LIFE!

Five: Thinking you're being punished.

For years, I thought God was punishing me by withholding my Boaz.

I couldn't figure out what I needed to do to get back into His good graces, so I did everything I could think of to be "good enough" to "deserve" a man.

Maybe there are some things you need to deal with, heal, and resolve before you can be in a relationship.

I no longer believe that God is punishing me by NOT giving me the one desire of my heart.

The truth is, I don't know when or if I'll ever meet my Mr. Right. I know some reasons why I am single, but even though I have addressed many of those issues, I'm still single. I wasted a lot of years trying to figure out WHY.

You're not being punished. God isn't mad at you. You don't have to be perfect to "deserve" a relationship. I don't know why you're single, but I do know that thinking you're in trouble with God completely messes up your mental and emotional well-being. Stop tormenting yourself!

If you're praying about it and the Lord is showing you some things you need to work on, do it. If not, you have to find ways to enjoy your life as a single person.

In an attempt to make peace with singleness, I have read books, blogs, posts, and reports. I've been to therapy, workshops, and conferences.

I've watched shows and videos, and listened to podcasts. I have learned how to be content and happy in my singleness.

Don't get me wrong: I would prefer a relationship! But I want to enjoy my life NOW whether or not Mr. Right is on his way.

Right now: stop making these mistakes! I promise, your life and your day will be more One-Derful!

How to Get Your Bounce Back

Sometimes, as a result of life's ups and downs, we find ourselves feeling like a partially deflated beach ball: not quite ruined, but devoid of our mojo (motivation and joy). Going through the motions with no real "bounce." Living, but not enjoying.

I recently went through one of these seasons.

One of my students interviewed me for an assignment in another class, and he asked me if I was happy. Honestly, I wasn't. And that bothered me - I wanted to get back into my happy place.

Here are 5 things that will help you get your bounce back.

Before I discovered these ideas for myself, I had to go through a time of healing.

During this time, I did some hiding and some soothing. Whether you are healing a physical wound, or an emotional or spiritual hurt, the concept is the same: you may have to scale back and rest.

Just like if you had the flu, you wouldn't jump out of bed and run a marathon - you would need some time to build up your strength. But, after a week or so, you might really be ready to get out of the house and resume normal activity.

These tips will help you once you've had a minute to rest and heal from the most acute pain - especially the non-physical variety.

1.   Meditation. It's been all over the news for a couple of years now, but meditation is a

practice that is thousands of years old. Every major religious and philosophical practice incorporates meditation. The way it was described to me is that prayer is when we talk to God; meditation is when we listen. Just five minutes per day in quiet meditation has been shown scientifically and anecdotally to improve mood, focus, and overall happiness. One of my teachers said, "If you don't have 5 minutes to meditate, you need to meditate for 30 minutes." There are many types of meditation, but you don't need a "type." Just sit with your eyes closed and breathe for five minutes and try to either clear your mind or count your breaths. It's that simple. Put the phone away, turn off the TV, and connect to your deepest self. This is where we are able to hear the "still, small voice" of God.

2. Journaling. I have been a consistent journal-keeper for 20 years now. It helps me to be able to process my thoughts and feelings, and allows me to go back and read and see how far I've come. You can safely express your emotions without worrying that you are burning out your friends or family. Journaling is a highly therapeutic way to work through situations that are difficult. Some days I write less than one page; some days I write many pages in many different sittings. Getting stuff out of my head and onto paper helps me bring order to any

emotional or mental clutter I am sorting through.

3.   Do what you must; enjoy what you can; table the rest. One of my girlfriends lost her mother a while back, and she felt guilty that she wasn't able to "show up fully" at work. A dedicated and conscientious worker, she felt like she was "slacking" compared to her normal full-tilt approach to her job. However, because she was already a high performer, her "slack" was still pretty good, and the truth was, nobody noticed except her! Sometimes you go through a season where you can't do it all with 100% focus or energy because you don't have that much to give. Do what you must. Get out of bed, feed the kids, get to work and do what NEEDS to be done. Don't volunteer for extra. Don't try to do all the things you normally do. Find things you can enjoy. Maybe it's a long-forgotten hobby, or going for a walk, or playing with your dog, or coloring with your child. Maybe it's just sitting and leafing through a magazine. Table the rest: I made a list - a literal, written list - of things I wasn't doing. Things that I wanted or needed to do, but was choosing not to. For example: iron napkins; reconsider social media strategy; update last will & testament; create new student event; buy new Christmas tree. This way, I didn't feel overwhelmed by random thoughts of what I "should" be doing. They were captured on paper for when I had my

bounce back and I could work on them when my mojo was restored. Turns out, some of the things took care of themselves....though, sadly, the napkins still need to be ironed.
4. Focus on what you HAVE and moving FORWARD. Granted, this is more difficult in practice than in theory. It's so easy to get focused on what we DON'T have - especially if we see others who have what we want. The Buddha posited that suffering comes from attachment to what we want and from not being content in our present state. Suffering, he said, doesn't come from our circumstances, but from our attachment to the way we want things to be. Less than 1,000 years later, St. Paul told us he had to "learn to be content in his present condition" (see Philippians 4:11-13). You have to make the choice to focus on what you have and where you are going. Jesus said no one who puts his (her) hand to the plow and looks backward is fit for service in God's kingdom (see Luke 9:62). Meaning: God cannot use you in your own life or anyone else's if you are still looking at what did or didn't happen. Remember Lot's wife? Salty.
5. Stop arguing with the past and the present. This one can be really tough. You will stay stuck as long as you cling to "what should have happened" or "what shouldn't have happened." Here's the deal: it happened (or didn't). Quit asking "why;" you may never know and even if you found out,

the answer probably wouldn't help you. If you can do something now, do it. If you can't, move on. "If he had done this; if she wouldn't have done that; if only I'd done it differently" - but he didn't, she did, and you did what you did. If you need to clean up something, do that, but then you must make peace with what happened. I'm not suggesting you have to like it, but you have to accept it, and acceptance requires doing what you can with what you have to move forward (see point number 4).

Life isn't always wonderful. You're going to go through difficult and painful seasons. But you can come out on the other side with something good to show for those seasons, and that's pretty One-Derful.

Consequences

It seems to me that we are in a culture where the idea of personal responsibility is fading into the past.

Of course, that's because nothing is your fault. You can blame anything you do or say (or don't do or don't say) on any number of things: how your parents raised you, the government, the economy, the media, mental and emotional struggles.

I'm not suggesting that these entities don't influence our behavior, but at the end of the day, we make choices and we engage in behavior.

We can choose our behavior. What we seem to forget is that when you engage in a behavior, you will experience a consequence.

I received an email from a student a few weeks ago. This student had earned a grade of D in the freshman business course. I say "earned" because my job as a teacher at a university is merely to record the grade the student earns.

The student emailed me because his grade point average had fallen below what it needed to be for him to keep his scholarship, and he wanted to know "if there was anything" I "could do" for him. In other words, would I please change his grade to increase his GPA.

Here's how you earn a D in a freshman class: don't attend class, or when you do attend, don't pay attention. Don't study. Don't do the homework (or don't turn it in on time). Don't pass the exams.

When I see you napping during class, I do not feel inspired to change your grade a few weeks later when you realize that your grades were too low. You chose to slack off – your grade reflects that. Behavior, meet Consequence.

We all do it: how many times have you been pulled over for speeding, and then you're telling your friends how that "jerk of a cop" had the nerve to write you a ticket?

Well, you were in a hurry. Never mind that you were in a hurry because you didn't manage your time well. If you choose to hit the snooze button, you're probably going to be late. That's not the police officer's fault.

I'm all for mercy and forgiveness, and we've all needed a second chance. But, the truth is, even when we are forgiven or we get a second chance, we frequently have to deal with lingering consequences.

A couple of years ago, I was in a VERY bad place. The relationship I thought was "the one" ended, and I was dealing with grief over the death of a close family member. I was at work, and couldn't get some of the office equipment to work properly. I was cursing and showing my butt – mostly beneath my breath. Unfortunately, one of my coworkers overheard me and went to the coworker (whom I have considered a friend for years) who manages the office, and repeated my comments to her. While it wasn't my intention, the repeated comments sounded like I was accusing her of not being able to do her job (keeping the equipment running).

This behind-the-back tale-telling deeply hurt my coworker and she let me know that she had heard about my comments. This gave me the opportunity to practice humbling myself and apologizing.

Fortunately, my coworker/friend is a Christian, and she did forgive me. We chit-chat from time-to-time, but two years later, I still feel a bit of lingering embarrassment over my behavior.

My first reaction was to be angry with the "idiot" who repeated my comments; but the real problem was me and my mouth. Behavior: mouth in drive while brain in park. Consequence: I damaged a friendship in less than 60 seconds that took me years to develop.

When you hurt someone's feelings or treat her badly, you are going to deal with some fallout.

Even if she forgives you, there may be lingering hurt there that has to heal.

If you accidentally run over my dog with your car, I may forgive you, and I may know that you didn't intend to kill my pet, but I'm still going to have to grieve that loss.

Nobody is perfect; we all make mistakes. We all say things we regret, keep silent when we should have spoken, do things we wish we could undo. Hopefully, we learn from these instances and learn to check our behavior or words.

Meanwhile, we have to learn to take responsibility and deal with consequences.

If you are negative and self-absorbed, people won't want to be around you. That is a consequence of your behavior.

If you are dishonest, people won't trust you.

If you are harsh and rude, you won't be invited out as much.

The tough thing about consequences is that sometimes you can't do anything to "fix" them. You just have to let the hurt feelings heal, pay the fee, replace the broken china, or whatever.

I think when we apologize, especially if the person forgives us, we think everything should be fine and nobody should have any lingering negative feelings. That isn't reality.

If you catch your husband cheating, you may forgive him and choose to stay and work on your marriage, but a normal reaction would be to not trust him right away.

One of my mentors, when I'm about to charge ahead with a behavior, reminds me to "play the song all the way through." Think about the consequences to myself and to the others involved. And, most importantly, take responsibility for those consequences.

A friend of mine recently lamented to me that he had driven drunk because "nobody took his keys." Are you kidding me? When you're in your 40's, nobody's taking your keys. If you drive drunk, that is 100% on you as a very bad decision. Don't blame it on work stress, unruly kids, or friends who don't wrestle you to the ground to take your car keys.

We choose our behavior and we can control it. If you are unable to control how you behave, then you are in for a lifetime of disaster. You do not get to separate consequences from behavior. You may get a lucky break – perhaps nothing bad results from your actions. But, there are only so many "free passes" from the Universe. Eventually, we all learn to take responsibility for our actions.

Play the song all the way through.

Fashionably Single

I love fashion.

To me, "fashion" is a term that represents the best face that can be presented. "Home fashion" depicts current decorating and design trends. "Fall (or Spring) fashion" tells us what's hot (and what's not) to wear.

In a small, Southern town, a single gal can feel like a fashion faux pas.

It feels like "everybody" is married (they aren't), and you're the only one who is alone (you're not). How can you feel like you're "in fashion" when your life seems so different from the people around you?

Here is your One-Derful Guide to Being Fashionably Single:

Get An Attitude. A positive one. Nobody wants to hear how hard it is to be single.

Your married friends either don't get it, or they're jealous of your freedom (ask them if you don't believe me).

You need to have one or two close friends with whom you can share your struggles, but try not to burn them out with your negativity. Otherwise, make it a point to not say anything negative about being single. You'll find you feel better.

I have had countless people stop me and tell me stories of a person they know who is bitter about singleness. The common denominator: they are tired of hearing it and don't want to set her (or him) up with anyone because they're so negative!

If you stay positive, you will stand out among other singles, which may help you get what you want: a date!

Be Confident. You don't have to *feel* confident, but *act* confident.

One way I've heard it is, "fake it 'til you make it." Look at those fashion models – they strut down the runway even when they topple off their 6-inch heels.

You have to wear singleness like a light garment – not a heavy blanket. Men will tell you that confidence is one of the sexiest accessories a woman can wear.

Use What You Have. The disheveled look is sometimes in vogue, but being unorganized is never pretty.

I believe that if you take care of what you have, you are demonstrating to the Universe that you are ready to handle more.

Look at the state of your environment: is your car tidy, or is it cluttered with papers, food wrappers, broken umbrellas, and other trash?

Imagine that you are in a parking lot or at the side of the road with car trouble and a nice, single man pulls over to help you. Or, you've had a first date with someone and he walks you to your car. When he peeks into the window, will he see a mess and think maybe you're not so "together?" Will he see a clean interior?

How about your home? You may not live in an expensive house. In fact, maybe you don't even own a home – perhaps you live in an apartment.

The point isn't the scale of your dwelling, the important thing is how do you live? Is your home tidy and clean? Are things put away? Can you find them? Men notice these details!

Furthermore, if you don't think you deserve to live in a clean place, how are you going to attract a mate who thinks you deserve the best?

Reflect What You Want. I used to have a wallet that had sentimental value to me. It was a gift, and over the years it had fallen apart to the point where I used a rubber band to hold it together.

One day, I asked myself, "is this the wallet of a prosperous, successful woman?" (No, it wasn't.)

You don't have to have a $500 designer wallet, but is the wallet you have in good repair? Is it neat and organized?

Why is this important? It's important because when you don't respect your money, why should the Universe give you more? When you're digging around in your messy handbag, looking for your 99-cent pen with no cap, do you look like someone who can handle a promotion?

One of the standard pieces of advice we give to young professionals is to "dress for the job you want, not the job you have."

Likewise, if you want better things and situations in your life, demonstrate to yourself, the Universe, and others that you deserve them.

I'm not telling you to go out and buy expensive things that you can't afford, but do the best you can NOW with what you have. It doesn't cost anything to organize your handbag!

Inventory Your Associations. Every year, you go through your closet or your kids' closets and you weed out the clothes that don't fit or are in poor repair.

Do the same with your friends, the organizations you are part of, and your relationships.

Just because you've been in a group for 5 years, doesn't mean you should continue. Are your relationships helping you today? Are they helping you be the woman you want to be? If not, let them go and make room for better things in your life.

I'd love to wear Chanel suits and carry Hermes bags; sadly, these items are not part of my lifestyle.

I've learned to create a fashionable look using a blend of inexpensive accessories, fine jewelry, designer pieces, and clothes from the clearance rack!

In the same way, you may prefer to be in a relationship, but if you're single, you can be the best single you possible! You may even find that your One-Derful Life actually attracts that special someone.

Even if it doesn't, you can still be fashionably and One-Derfully single!

Get Your Freedom!

I owned my own home (by myself!) for eighteen years.

For at least the last 5 years, I frequently joked that I fantasized about returning to renting because I was overwhelmed and tired of the burden of home ownership.

More than once, I seriously considered selling the house, but would always decide to focus on more pressing projects.

However, one January, I contacted a Realtor "just to see" what my options were. Well, to make a fairly short story even shorter, we listed the house and only 10 days later had a contract for my full asking price!

Many of my friends questioned the soundness of this decision. After all, I teach business and have consulted many individuals and businesses regarding profitable financial strategies.

It's true that I no longer have an asset associated with my monthly housing costs, but I also have no debt whatsoever, and I do have something even more valuable to me than a house: I have my freedom. (By the way: many of my girlfriends' husbands have lauded my decision and wistfully dream about the free time I describe now that I don't have a lawn, a roof, or a crawlspace.)

For me, owning a house by myself was a constant exercise in anxiety (what's going to go wrong next?), overwhelm (there's always some major repair or upgrade that needs to be done), and loneliness (a constant reminder that I had a house with a yard, but no husband, no family and no children).

I reached a point where I decided freedom was more valuable to me than this one asset.

Maybe selling a house isn't part of your quest for freedom, but I believe most people want to feel free.

We want more money because we think it will bring freedom; we want freedom to do what we want to do without being judged; we even want to feel free to eat whatever we like without gaining weight.

Regardless of your specific desires, here are some areas where we can all use some more freedom:

1. Freedom from constraint. For me, the house was like a 1,700 square foot anchor. It required a lot of time and money to keep up the house, and I didn't enjoy the constant repairs and projects that were endlessly piling up. It had become more of a burden than a blessing; more weights than wings. What is your anchor? Maybe it's a job where you feel stuck or a relationship where you aren't valued. Maybe it's fear of speaking your truth or worry that you'll be judged if you follow your heart's desire. Before you just "cast off" whatever you feel is constraining you, be sure that the costs actually outweigh the benefits. But if they do, start taking

the steps to free yourself from what is constraining you.

2. Freedom from clutter. You've heard this one a thousand times before, right? But clutter really does enslave us. And not just physical clutter (like those closets that need to be cleaned out) – how about relationships in your life that you have outgrown? How about the health issues you aren't dealing with? How about the debt or the dust bunnies or the debilitating mental dialogue that is constantly dragging you down and stealing your energy? What is no longer serving you that you need to get rid of?

3. Freedom from confusion. God is not a God of confusion, but of order and peace (see 1 Corinthians 14:33). It's easy to feel confused because we have so much information coming at us all the time. Eat dairy no, don't eat dairy! Get a certain health test every year – wait, it's not necessary! Stay out of the sun – or, make sure you're getting some sun because you need the vitamin D. Then there are the endless opinions from news outlets, social media, and the latest "thought leaders." Tips, hacks, and shortcuts that are supposed to make your life easier can just make you feel like you're not doing enough, and you're not good at whatever you ARE doing. Don't know what to do about something? Follow peace – that's

how the Holy Spirit leads us. Not sure you have a peaceful leading yet? Here's some advice that helps me: when in doubt, don't. Wait until you have peace and clarity. If you ask God for clarity, wisdom, and guidance – He will give it to you because He gives wisdom liberally when we ask for it (see James 1:5). God is not the author of confusion (again, see 1 Corinthians 14:33), so if your mind is spinning over "what to do," that is NOT from the Lord!

4. Freedom from conflict. Having running gun battles with yourself, God, or other people steals your energy and your ability to enjoy your life and for others to enjoy being around you! "But you don't know what they did to me," you may cry. I hear you. But if having the same conversation (or argument) with yourself, others, or God isn't producing results, STOP! This isn't to say you shouldn't bring good, Godly correction when needed. But stop fighting to have your way all the time. Forgiveness is a mindset and a behavior, not an emotion. You will almost never "feel like" forgiving someone, but if you want to feel free, you will have to do it.

My freedom is an asset I can't put a value on - it is priceless. And I wouldn't trade it for anything.

Grace's Anatomy

I've constantly working to up-level many areas of my life. Most of my mentors and role models exhibit a trait I've heard referred to as "graciousness."

I've heard about grace in context of faith - God's unmerited favor - but I never really understood what being a gracious woman would look like. So I did some investigating!

Merriam-Webster defines "gracious" as, "Courteous, kind, pleasant."

I love that, because it seems like our current culture rewards behavior that is discourteous, unkind, and unpleasant.

It's in vogue to slam people on social media. Complaining is "venting." Being rude is "keeping it real."

I think a truly gracious woman is one who is courteous, kind, and pleasant even when the other person doesn't "deserve" it, which would echo the traditional understanding of God's grace - His unmerited favor.

I'm not talking about letting people walk over you, or being a doormat with a pretty hairstyle. But, speaking to that coworker that you don't really like (I mean, would it really kill you to say, "Good morning" when you pass her in the hallway?). Or, asking the cashier how she's doing even if she grunts in reply. Or, being nice when you call to complain about the mistake on the phone bill.

Yes, you may need to be clear and bring correction, but that old saying, "You draw more flies with honey than with vinegar" applies. Not that I'm trying to attract flies, mind you. You can always be nasty if being courteous, kind, and pleasant doesn't do the trick. But you can almost never go from nasty to nice with your integrity intact.

Gracious women let people off the hook. Again, I'm not suggesting you give people a pass when they're using and abusing you. But people make mistakes.

Now, if it's the same "mistake" two or three times, you may be looking at a pattern - and that's a completely different issue. Especially if someone apologizes to you - can you let it go?

One of my friends is angry because he feels like his girlfriend wasn't supportive of him 5 years ago when he started his business. They broke up and are now "working it out," but he still goes back to his resentment of her lack of support.

My advice: let her off the hook and give her the opportunity to be supportive or end the relationship permanently. It's not fair to make her keep begging for forgiveness. Also, if you give her the chance to support you and you feel like she doesn't give you what you need, you can end things at that point.

Be willing to give people a chance.

St. Paul said in 1 Corinthians that "Love keeps no account," in other words, love doesn't keep score.

Most married folk will tell you that if your partner is constantly bringing up the mistakes you made in the past, it's hard to move forward.

When we keep score against others, we are setting up a win-lose situation where we want to win, and that means they must lose. But nobody wants to lose - it feels bad.

If you want to keep track of something, keep track of the good things the person brings into your life. If you look at the relationship and feel it is out-of-balance, maybe it's time to end it. Or, pull back and give them the space to invest.

When you're doing something to get something, that's not love. That's manipulation. When you're keeping track of all the things you've done (notice how we only count our good deeds, not our bad ones?) and pointing out what they HAVEN'T done, it's clear that you're only giving to get. When you're truly giving out of love, it feels good to you and the person's reciprocity is not your top priority.

A gracious woman forgives. This one is tough. Forgiveness is never deserved - the very definition means that a debt is being wiped away as if it was never there. Nobody "deserves" forgiveness.

A Course in Miracles says we can have a resentment or we can have a miracle - but we cannot have both.

Forgiveness is not the same as reconciliation. When you forgive someone, it doesn't mean you're going to be friends again. You may not speak again.

When you forgive, you are wiping the slate clean of their past actions toward you. This doesn't mean you need to give them another chance, it just means you're moving on.

You've heard that when you forgive someone, it releases you, not them. I've found this to be true. And difficult. I'm an Olympic-level grudge carrier. But that weight just gets heavier as time goes on. Then, you're angry and bitter and resentful, and you wonder why you don't feel grateful or peaceful or happy. How could you, weighed down as you are with the grievances over behavior the other person has long since forgotten. Focused on the past, how can you see the opportunities or blessings that are here now?

Here's a simple prayer I learned from Marianne Williamson to pray every time I start replaying the mental tape of someone's "sin:" "(Insert person's name here), I forgive you and I release you to the Holy Spirit."

If you have to say it 50 times a day, do it. It will break your thought patterns, and it will help alchemize your emotions (in the words of Marianne Williamson). Meaning, your hurt feelings will begin to feel soothed and will eventually be replaced with a feeling of peace.

I'm certainly not where I want to be on the graciousness scale, but at least I'm not where I used to be.

I know I've lived a lot of years with resentment and unforgiveness, and I want peace and happiness instead. That's more of the One-Derful Life I want for myself.

4 Guys to Avoid

I have recently concluded an 18-month stint of online dating, which I (mostly) enjoyed. During that time, I met some terrific men.

I also met some gentlemen that I feel are the types of fellas you may want to avoid. They're not bad people, but if you're looking for a serious relationship, these guys will waste your time.

I have created names for these archetypes to better describe the characteristics. Allow me to introduce them:

Pat. This is a nod to the ambiguous, asexual "Saturday Night Live" character: male or female? The Pat probably isn't gay, and he probably isn't interested in being a woman.

He is, however, a highly feminized male. To be fair, there are men who truly have become more feminized biologically. Obesity increases estrogen production, which decreases testosterone.

Additionally, the xenoestrogens in our environment and food supply can have the effect of increasing estrogen in the body.

All that aside, the Pat desires to be the female in the relationship. If you are a strong, assertive woman who likes to take the lead, the Pat is the perfect guy for you!

If you're old-fashioned and want someone who will "wear the pants" in the relationship, you're going to be confused and frustrated by the Pat.

The Pat has feminine energy; again, I am not saying he is homosexual!

Feminine energy is receptive, responsive, and magnetic; male energy is instigating, proactive, and assertive.

We all have both, but the Pat's feminine energy makes him the antithesis of the traditional, alpha male – which isn't necessarily a bad thing!

But, if you want a man who will pursue you, stand up for you, and take the lead, the Pat will disappoint you.

He'll wait for you to suggest plans, call him, and drive the relationship.

If that's the case, plan to ditch him and drive somewhere you can meet a more masculine man.

Mitch. The Mitch is not as systemically feminized as the Pat, but he will have a flair for the overdramatic.

The Mitch will literally pout, cry, and manipulate to get his way.

He tends to be moody, controlling, and suspicious. He may accuse you of cheating on him, lying to him, or doing things that have no basis in reality.

When you confront the behavior, he will blame you for his actions.

The Mitch needs a lot of attention; however, if you give him too much attention, he will complain that he feels smothered.

Indeed, it is very difficult to make him happy.

He can be incredibly oversensitive, and will analyze everything you say and do (and don't say and don't do), and will then pick fights with you based on the information he has gleaned.

He will establish inappropriate connections with your friends and family, and will try to employ them in manipulating you so that he can get his way.

If you like emotional roller coasters, this guy is Prince Charming! If not, he's Prince Alarming – block him on social media, cut off all contact, and don't keep trying to "work it out" because you'll never be able to fill the Mitch's emotional black hole.

Mad Max. As the name implies, Mad Max is just angry.

He's a victim most of the time, and nothing is his fault.

He's been wronged at work, in love, by the government, by his family, and by God.

At first, you think you're smoothing his ruffled feathers and creating an Us against Them bubble in which the two of you are pilot and co-pilot – flying the unfriendly skies, but flying united.

In reality, it is only a matter of time before all that anger gets focused on YOU.

He may not want to break up with you, but everything that doesn't go to his liking (or yours) will be your fault – never his.

Mad Max holds on to the wounds of his past and won't let go of resentments because they are so integral to his identity.

If you're a fixer, you think you can save him and heal him, but he'll just end up resenting you because you "don't understand what it's been like."

If you like going to therapy and being an emotional scapegoat, Mad Max is the guy for you!

Otherwise, give him a real reason to be mad at you: dump him and find a guy who knows how to deal with life.

X: This guy's name doesn't really matter, because the only name you'll ever hear will be the name of his ex-wife, ex-fiancee, or ex-girlfriend.

By the end of the first date, you will know more about X's ex than you will about him!

He'll know virtually nothing about you, because he spent the entire time talking about "her."

But, he'll be enchanted by you because you spent the entire date listening to him.

If you're like me, every time he compares you to the ex, you'll feel smug and superior because you're "winning." I mean, he clearly thinks you're great and she was a loser, right?

However, you're missing the point: he's still talking about her. People talk about what they're thinking about. And men don't multitask mentally like women do; if he's talking about her, he's thinking about her, and he's not thinking about you.

At the very least, he doesn't even respect you enough to shut up about his ex, her family, her drama, and their relationship long enough to plug into the present moment with YOU.

If you are on a first or second date with someone and know his ex's name, occupation, how and when they met, how and why they broke up, and her present life situation, you have met X.

He's probably a nice guy, but he's hung up on her – even though he will SWEAR he's over her and he'd NEVER take her back, even if she begged.

There is not room in X's heart or life for you.

If you're into emotional threesomes, and enjoy other people's drama, X is a great catch.

Otherwise, catch the next train out of Ex-ville and meet someone who's interested in YOU!

If you want a One-Derful life, you don't want to waste your precious time and energy on these guys – be on the lookout for anyone who's going to cast you in a supporting role in his tacky drama, and keep it moving!

There are lots of great men out there, but you won't meet them if you're spending time with these guys!

Get Your Space Together!

Regardless of your relationship status, you probably want to feel more peaceful, more focused, and better able to receive good things into your life.

Maybe it's a bit of a cliché, but I have bought into the idea that what we see on the outside is a representation of what's going on inside. In other words, a cluttered home or office may be indicative of a mess somewhere in our hearts or minds.

I have found it incredibly helpful and supportive to keep my environment as ordered as possible; meaning, I strive to keep my home, my office, my car, and even my handbag neat and tidy and clean.

Don't get me wrong: my spaces aren't perfect, but drop by my house or office unannounced, and I won't be embarrassed. (That's not an invitation – merely an example.)

To me, there's nothing more disappointing than seeing a beautiful luxury car in a parking lot and moving in for a closer look, only to find the inside littered with takeout food containers, gym clothes, and scattered papers.

My mom is a very neat and organized person, and while I aspire to her level of neatness, decluttering and tidying up have not come easily for me.

However, as I have learned to clear the clutter and let go of old "stuff," I have become more peaceful, focused, and able to focus on other areas of my life.

"Why does it even matter?" you may ask.

First, the most practical reason to get your space clean and organized: it saves you time and energy because you can find things.

If you've ever spent hours looking for a misplaced item or if you've been late getting out the door because you couldn't find things, you know it would be faster if you could locate whatever you need: stamps (does anyone actually mail anything anymore?), keys, kids' shoes, phone charger.

Have you ever been behind someone in the grocery store checkout line who can't find her debit card in her mess of a handbag?

If you have to spend 20 minutes looking for your bills before you can even pay them, you've expended time and energy that you need to attend to your finances, but also that you could use for something fun later on!

Second, if you want to have a man in your life, you need to know that most men appreciate order.

This will elicit audible guffaws from our married readers who will swear that their husbands have zero interest in keeping the house tidy. Which is actually true: most men have little interest in domestic chores, but most have a high need for domestic support (see the book *His Needs, Her Needs* by Dr. Willard F. Harley).

I'm not saying it should be 100% the woman's responsibility to keep a home neat, but even working mothers find that they do the majority of the work at home when it comes to chores.

You may wonder at the fact that a man will spend hours washing and polishing his vehicle, but can't be bothered to wipe off the kitchen counter. This is because he values his vehicle and therefore he takes care of it.

A great way to inspire a man to buy you things you want (or more things or better things) is by taking care of what you already have.

I always say, "I may not have the most expensive possessions, but I take the absolute best care of them that I can."

Men don't want you feverishly dusting the furniture and mopping the floor, but it's nice to come home to an orderly environment.

If you've ever had a housekeeper, isn't it wonderful to walk in the house just hours after she's finished? You deserve that, and so does your family.

Third, when you order your environment, you are making a statement to the Universe that you deserve a peaceful life and ordered surroundings.

Of course, nobody gets a pass on suffering, and we're all going to have to deal with situations and circumstances that rob us of peace and stifle our joy.

That's why controlling what you can is so useful: it provides us with a way to have order and clarity when life doesn't make sense.

Many people report a therapeutic benefit to clearing away clutter – it can be a helpful way to let go of the past or bring closure to difficult seasons.

In the same way you wouldn't go from never working out to running a 5k, don't go whole-hog trying to get your spaces organized all at once. I like to suggest starting with your handbag.

Marla Cilley, The FlyLady, says start with the kitchen sink.

Either way: it's something small and you can see and appreciate the immediate results.

Don't tackle the entire dresser; just organize ONE drawer.

I like *The Life Changing Magic of Tidying Up* by Marie Kondo, but her method of piling up ALL of your clothes in the middle of the floor and sorting through them in one session is way too overwhelming to me.

I prefer to address one section of the closet or one drawer at the time.

There are a lot of different ways to shell this peanut – find one that works for you and just do a little bit each day. If you have kids who are over the age of 5, they can go through their own clothes or toys and find ones they don't wear or like that someone else could have (especially if "Santa Claus won't bring any new toys unless there's room for them").

Have 15 minutes at work before your next call? Don't numb out on social media; instead, clean out a desk drawer or a set of files. You'll feel more productive and energetic, and you'll probably come up with some good ideas because the creative part of your brain is available to work because the rest of your brain is busy with the routine task of sorting paper clips.

Just try making some small adjustments in your environment and see if you don't feel more One-Derful and a little bit more peaceful.

I Can Do This

A lot of people quote Philippians 4:13 ("I can do all things through Christ") as a justification for doing whatever they want to do. I like how the Amplified Bible translates the verse: "I have strength for all things in Christ who empowers me – I am ready for anything and equal to anything through Him who infuses inner strength into me; I am self-sufficient in Christ's sufficiency."

This verse has taken on new meaning for me. When I am struggling with loneliness and very deep feelings of sadness, any holiday tends to set me back.

Easter Sunday one year was very difficult for me because it's a time for family and celebration, and I don't have a family. While Easter is the most important day in my religion, I mostly was focused on the sudden resurrection of my depression. I spent most of the day in a very bad mental space, feeling alone and sorry for myself.

The part of Philippians 4:13 that struck me on that day was "I have strength for all things in Christ who empowers me – I am ready for anything..."

I realized that if God's plan for my life is for me to be single, He is giving me (already – not going to give me someday) the grace, strength, and ability to live life alone and to enjoy it and live fully and abundantly.

I must admit that this revelation did not instantly erase my loneliness or sad feelings, but it did give me a sense of hope that the Lord has equipped me NOW to live life with joy and peace (hello, One-Derful Life!).

Those tools are currently sitting in my emotional toolbox. I should not keep saying, "I just can't stand this," "I can't imagine being alone forever," or, "I'm doomed to feel this way for the rest of my life."

Jesus said, "With man this is impossible, but with God all things are possible." It is true that left to my own resources and devices, it is impossible for me to have peace and joy when my circumstances aren't what I want them to be.

But what's the point of being a Believer if I'm not going to BELIEVE that God is with me, helping me, and planning a good life for me?

If God only saves us so we can barely get by and survive until we die and go to heaven, why would anyone want to be saved? What kind of witness is it when we're just barely getting by, trudging and moping and miserable?

As I meditated on this idea for the next week or so, I started to feel more peaceful and comforted.

God promises never to allow more than we can bear, and He will always provide the solution with the problem.

I also like the part of Philippians 4:13 that says, "I am equal to anything." I don't have to feel inferior because of any situation.

For me, it's my marital status and lack of family. For others I know, it's not having a college education, unemployment, infertility, financial problems, or health issues.

I don't need to give in to the fear that I'm "less than" because I'm alone.

Every year, I attend a banquet where I work. I enjoy it, but this year I felt anxious and depressed, and didn't know if I was up to the evening. I always find it strange that I feel lonely, but the loneliness just makes me want to stay home alone. Doesn't make sense.

I prayed and asked the Lord to help me enjoy myself and feel "a part of," rather than "apart from." I do want to clarify that my feelings have nothing to do with my colleagues. I work with many kind, friendly, fun people – they never make me feel unwelcome.

I really had an amazing evening. I was walking in, and 3 of my coworkers joined me (so I didn't have to walk in alone), then I parked myself with several of my friends during the pre-dinner reception, and I was invited to sit at a table with some of my favorite people.

Afterwards, I was invited to a party (which I attended) where I spent the evening laughing with some of my favorite colleagues. I just wanted to get through the evening, but God provided me an abundance of fun people and a feeling of belonging.

This showed me that He will send me what I need, when I need it, if I ask Him, do my part, and be positive.

Of course, I still wish my circumstances would change, but everybody has circumstances they would like to see changed. What I'm focusing on right now is that God has given me the ability to have a One-Derful Life, enjoy that life, and have peace and joy RIGHT NOW. I can have a great life even if I am single, even if I have no family, and even if I sometimes feel lonely.

Now I will go to the gym, because it turns out that eating 14 chocolate bunnies and a peepload of Peeps was not such a great way to deal with Easter depression.

Let Go

I recently heard Dr. Henry Cloud speak about his book, *Necessary Endings.*

If you're not familiar with Dr. Cloud, he is a Christian clinical psychologist and author – I highly recommend his book *Boundaries*, if you need to learn to have healthier relationships in every area of your life.

Dr. Cloud's talk was focused around the idea that you cannot carry every relationship, belief, and behavior from your present into your future – especially if you want a future that is different from your past or your present.

I heard a different example once: when Tarzan is swinging through the jungle, he has to LET GO of the vine behind him before he can move forward on the vine in front of him.

Endings are scary to me. Whether it's the end of a dating relationship, a friendship, a job, or a season of life, I fear endings. I think I fear them because the unknown makes me feel anxious. Also, endings are sad, and I fear feeling sad.

Given my resistance to endings, it doesn't really make sense that my favorite holiday is New Year's.

But I love the feeling of a new start and a clean slate. I love reviewing the past year and seeing if I achieved any of my goals, as well as setting new goals for the year to come.

Recently, I've been wondering if I could apply that same excitement about the end of the year to other endings.

Bear with me through this example: if I knew my life would be over on December 31, I'm sure I wouldn't be so excited about the end of the year.

Sadly, I tend to see other endings as permanent – maybe that's why they're scary.

People say, "When God closes one door, He opens another," but it's the waiting in the hallway for the other door to open that I dread.

However, I have learned that the blessing is frequently found in the hallway. It's a time to focus, breathe, rest, and prepare for that next door to open.

Here's what it looks like for me: we've always had a certain type of relationship, so we have to have that in the future.

Or, I've been involved in a certain project since the beginning, and I have to stick with it.

Then there's my personal favorite: I need things to be a particular way so I'll be okay. This is a problem because I can't carry everything from my past into my future – I want a new future.

Dr. Cloud says that "just because you've been doing something for a long time, doesn't mean you're supposed to keep doing it."

That was a revelation to me. I believe in being committed to people and projects, but sometimes it's time to let go.

Maybe someone else is supposed to have the experience, or maybe God wants to take me to a new place, but He can't do it because I'm still clinging to that vine behind me.

How do you know when it's time to let go?
For me, I believe the Holy Spirit leads us with a
sense of peace.

I try not to make decisions out of fear, because
it's been my experience that God doesn't teach
me through fear (exception: fear of snakes and
bugs). He leads me with a sense of peace.

I was involved in an organization for many,
many years. I was responsible for founding it,
and have remained a dedicated leader.

Recently, the group experienced a lot of
upheaval and drama. At first, I would not
consider stepping back; I mean, it was "MY
GROUP." I started it.

The drama unfolded over several days, and at
one point I woke up in the middle of the night
with a clear thought: I need to resign my position
in the organization. And, I had peace about it,
which I had not experienced previously.

I wasn't really sure if this was guidance from
the Holy Spirit, or a knee-jerk reaction to the
drama, so I waited 24 hours to take action.

When I resigned, I felt a true, deep peace and
relief that surprised me. I haven't regretted my
decision, and being away from the drama and
negativity have been good for my soul.

I believe God wants us to travel lightly through
this life. I tend to want to haul around all of the
baggage I've accumulated in life, but I think God
would prefer that we only take what we need.

Isn't that what Jesus instructed his disciples to
do when he sent them out to witness? Take only
what you need. Leave the gun, take the cannoli

(you've seen "The Godfather," right?). Leave the resentment, take the good memories. Leave the status, take the experience. Leave the toxicity, take the love.

Buddhists meditate on the idea of bringing an empty rice bowl to the Universe. In Tibet, Buddhist monks will walk through town in the morning with an empty rice bowl, and the villagers fill it with rice –that is how the monks get their food.

They have faith that their daily bread will indeed be provided, but only if the bowl is empty. And the villagers are excited to fill those bowls because they feel blessed to feed and care for the monks. I love that image! There's no room for God to fill my rice bowl if it's not empty.

I wonder if prayers seem to be "unanswered" because we ask God for something, but we haven't made room in our lives for what we're requesting. That's the necessary ending – forgetting what lies behind and being available to embrace the new thing He wants to give us.

Maybe He wants to give us a new way of thinking, a new way of feeling, a new relationship, a healed relationship, a new opportunity or experience. But if we're clutching onto the old, how can we take hold of the new?

Ask Him to show you what needs to end. Maybe it's a friendship, a behavior, a habit, a relationship.

Remember, "end" can mean "change." The caterpillar changes into a butterfly. Leave the old, take the new. It's a One-Derful new way of living.

Get Your Physical Life Together

Whether your definition of success means being the best stay-at-home mom, being a corporate wiz, or being an award-winning teacher, you need the physical strength, stamina, and energy to be able to manage your life. (Spoiler alert: the older you get, the less energy you have even if you are exercising and eating right!)

Look at any wildly successful CEO and you will find that he or she makes time for exercise and sleep, and chooses water and whole, "real" foods much of the time.

Not only do you need the physical stamina to do what you need to do physically (like going to meetings, chasing a toddler, or cleaning up the den), you need to be feeling well physically in order to function well mentally and emotionally.

When your body is feeling yucky – whether you're sick, recovering from a late night of celebrating, or nursing a food "hangover" – you feel slow and sluggish mentally.

Not to mention the emotional toll of beating yourself up because you're unhappy with your weight or you feel embarrassed by your appearance.

It's not about being a particular dress size or looking like a model (or your group fitness instructor), it's about looking and feeling the way that makes you feel good about yourself and able to do what you need to do.

Since I'm not a health coach or qualified fitness expert, and because that information is so widely and readily available, I want to focus on HOW your physical health and wellness affect your life and WHY you need this area to be "on fleek" (on point, put together, working correctly) in order to feel great and live your own One-Derful Life.

I have learned that my energy levels are very much tied into what I eat.

For me, if I binge on sugar on Sunday, I will pay on Monday in the form of bloating, puffiness, mental sluggishness, and irritability.

I will literally feel hungover, even though I haven't had any alcohol or drugs in more than 20 years. Not everybody feels that way. (Of course, not everybody will snarfle up an entire package of Oreos in 37 minutes flat. Okay, it doesn't really take me that long. But I digress...)

I used to exercise to punish myself either after eating too much, or just to generally abuse myself because I was dissatisfied with my appearance.

Today, I exercise because I want to take care of myself and I know it helps me feel good.

When I exercise, I get my brain chemistry producing feel-good hormones, I feel confident, and I feel like I have accomplished something.

You don't have to run a 5k or be the best Zumba dancer – just move your body!

Taking care of yourself physically is the equivalent of putting your own oxygen mask on first on an airplane. This well-worn analogy reminds us that we must take care of ourselves in order to be able to care for others.

If I don't have the physical energy and mental acuity to help my college students, I won't be of much service to them.

If I'm not taking care of my body, I won't have the ability to stay mentally focused and emotionally calm when life throws me a curveball.

There are a lot of products and programs out there that can help you get your physical life together.

You have to find what works best for you, but the basics should include 7-9 hours of sleep (in a row, at night); lots of clean water to drink; physical movement; clean, healthy food; and, regular checkups with your doctor, dentist, and other healthcare professionals. (Please ALWAYS consult with your healthcare team before you start any diet or exercise program to be sure it will be right for you.)

Physical health gives you the confidence and energy you need to live your own One-Derful Life.

If you want to be successful at anything, you need to have the physical and mental ability to perform, and that requires that you take responsibility and intentional action toward your own optimal health.

I believe in "progress, not perfection," so don't try to change everything all at once. Just do one thing today that would support your physical health.

Even if it's a walk around the block or Googling, "healthy meals."

Regardless of your age, you WILL feel more One-Derful if you take responsibility for your body and start with small changes that you can sustain.

I Wish

I've been thinking about jealousy a lot lately. Or, lately I've realized I have a problem with jealousy.

This line of thought began a few weeks ago. I was watching one of my favorite reality shows (I'm too embarrassed to tell you which one), and I started wondering why one of the women on the show has such a fantastic boyfriend.

I started out jokingly asking the Lord, "Hey – do You have another one of those?" Then, I asked, "Lord, what's up? Here's a woman that doesn't seem to care anything about You, or even care about being honest and kind to others, and she has a really great guy who loves her. And, here I am, trying to obey You, trying to live for You, and I keep getting the fuzzy end of the lollipop."

As I listened to myself, I realized I wasn't joking, I wasn't even merely curious. I was jealous.

I'm a very competitive person, and sometimes that's a good thing, but it also has caused me to compare myself to others.

Have you ever noticed we tend to compare ourselves to people that have what we want, rather than people who don't?

I will compare myself to celebrities, friends, people in the community, but never to women starving in Africa or being persecuted in the Middle East.

Maybe the reason we don't compare ourselves to people who are less fortunate than we are is because we know we'll feel guilty for being so shallow.

Nobody likes to admit she's jealous. It sounds terrible, doesn't it? After all, "Do Not Covet" is the Tenth of the Ten Commandments.

Let's rephrase it for today's culture: "You shall not be jealous or envious or wish you had anybody else's house, her husband, her kids, her car, her figure, her job, her money, her education, or ANYTHING that somebody else has." ANYTHING. And you're not excused just because YOU think she doesn't deserve what she has.

Ouch. Now sensitive to my own jealousy, I started noticing other areas where I'm jealous.

For example, a friend of mine was selected at her job to go on a business trip to France recently. I love France. One morning, my mind was wandering, and it wandered onto the path of "How come she gets a cool trip to France and I don't?" (In whiny voice: it's not fair.)

Fortunately, this time I caught myself and was able to stop my mind in its tracks. If the Lord had wanted me to go to France, He would have arranged for me to be selected at MY job for a trip to France.

If I were supposed to be in France, I would be in France. And, being upset and jealous isn't going to magically transport me to France.

Plus, the reason I'd want to go to France is that France makes me happy. So, I can skip the jet lag and decide to be happy without packing a bag.

Of course, then I felt like the Holy Spirit told me I'd better pray for my friend – that she's enjoying her trip and having fun. I did it out of obedience, but I actually felt a little bit better afterwards.

Why do other people get what you want? Why do you pray and believe for something and then watch an "ungodly" or "undeserving" person (in our opinion – I'll be writing on my problems with being judgmental in a later tome) get what you've been hoping for? What's the point of trying to live according to Christian principles when you watch your friends who don't care about (or even despise) God being blessed? (Read Malachi 3:14 for the answer to this question.)

Here's what I have learned:

If you're serving God to GET something, your motives are not godly (see James 4:3).

If you're looking at anybody else's life (or stuff) and you're miffed, irritated, or angry that God hasn't given you THAT, you are saying you know better than God about what you should have, and that is pride.

If you have decided you cannot be happy unless you have THAT (house, husband, kids, money, car, figure, etc.), you are practicing idolatry.

Let's recap: ungodly motives, pride, and idolatry. That's what I've been guilty of, and that scares me.

Recently, my pastor was imitating the attitude we have sometimes: "Listen here, God. Clearly,

You don't know what you're doing when it comes to my life, so I'll just take over."

He was going overboard to make his point, but I realized that in my case, it was not a joke – that's the attitude I've had. This is scary to me because I've tried things MY way (they didn't turn out so well).

The reason to serve God isn't to get what you want.

God isn't a Divine Vending Machine where you put in your hard work and get to choose the treat that comes rolling off the shelf.

If you're going to be happy in life, you have to get comfortable with unanswered questions.

You have to be doing the right thing because it's the right thing and that's who you are; otherwise, you'll always feel like you're doing "your part" and God is dropping the ball.

Jealousy hurts YOU. Being angry because somebody else has something you don't think she deserves hurts YOU.

That's hard to hear, but it's the truth, and I have to stop that behavior because that kind of hurt will keep you out of peace and happiness 100% of the time.

I think it's normal human behavior to see others and think, "I wish I had that." If we follow that thought up with, "Well, if the Lord has that for me, I'll get it in His time," we're probably okay.

Also, if you're jealous of someone else, but you're not willing to do what she did to get what she has, maybe it's not God's fault you don't have what she has.

Trying to figure out WHY she has this and you don't, and trying to understand WHY you've believed for that and she got it without even being a Believer will make you insane.

You're not going to figure it out, and you're not going to get what you want from God by throwing a spiritual (or actual) temper tantrum (I know – I've tried).

We need to crucify our jealousy this month. I promise you, it will want to have multiple resurrections, but we have to keep laying it at the foot of the cross.

If you want to feel better about your life, turn on the news and see how women in other countries live – you'll see how blessed we are here. And you'll treasure your One-Derful Life.

A One-Derful Life Plan

One fall, I attended the local Chamber of Commerce Annual Membership Luncheon. The keynote speaker was Ms. Darla Moore – one of my she-roes and someone I very much respect and admire.

Ms. Moore spoke about the great strides being made in the local area in terms of economic development and how that process can be adopted to other locales, leading to greater success in this great state of ours.

As a pro-business, capitalism-loving educator, I certainly appreciated her comments as they were intended: to inspire economic development.

However, she also inspired me as I took her comments to heart on a personal level. I believe her plan for economic success holds some gems for personal success. So, I would like to dedicate this chapter to Ms. Darla Moore and give her full credit for these ideas.

Her opening statement was, "Nobody's coming to help us. We have to help ourselves." That is so true for us singles!

Many times we think there's a Prince Charming coming to save us from our bills and our lives and our very selves.

Certainly, a partnership does involve helping each other, but most men are not looking for a woman who is a walking disaster.

You have to get your finances, your emotions, and your life in order if you want to attract a man who has his finances, emotions, and life in order.

Be a "good thing." Besides, didn't God say He is your Help? Reach out to Him first.

Ms. Moore went on to highlight four keys to "saving ourselves:" a vision, being realistic about our assets, having short- and long-term plans, and good relationships with willing partners.

A vision. You have to know what you want for your life. "If what you are doing doesn't work, try something else," Ms. Moore said.

She also advised that small, incremental changes won't always get you the results you want; sometimes you have to make radical changes if you want radical results.

In life, sometimes you have to make drastic changes if you want to see dramatic results.

Take a realistic inventory of your assets. We can all come up with a list of our failures or what isn't working in our lives.

If you have a "failure" in your past (and we all do), there's nothing you can do to change that; however, you can do something to avoid failing in that area in the future.

I was dating someone and later found out he was cheating on me the entire time we were together.

In hindsight, I saw red flags but I chose to ignore them because I wanted the relationship to work.

There's nothing I can do about that relationship now; however, I can be sure not to ignore warning signs – I can promise you I won't be played out like that again!

Everyone has something they can work with – maybe you have great looks or a winning smile or a unique sense of humor.

If you're single, maybe you have the freedom to move somewhere else or the ability to explore some new interests.

Have a short-term plan and a long-term plan. If your long-term desire is to get married and have a family, it is unlikely you will meet your husband while sitting on your couch night after night (unless you're giving online dating a shot).

You have to have a short-term plan of action that supports your long-term plan. Get out there and meet people: ask friends to set you up, go where people are, try online dating – you have to do something different if you want different results.

I'm all for spontaneity, but you also have to have direction if you want to achieve that vision for your life.

You need good relationships with willing partners. You need people. You need friends; you need to be able to get along with people.

Someone who likes you may set you up with a nice fella. The key is, people won't introduce you to a NICE fella if they don't like YOU.

Partnerships are successful when both parties bring something of value to the relationship.

Are you bringing value to your coworkers, your employer, your family, your friends?

I've had men ask me on dates what I'm "bringing to the party," and they're not talking about my tried-and-true red velvet cupcakes.

One of Ms. Moore's key points was about the importance of education. That, too, translates into a powerful life lesson.

Formal education is valuable and I encourage you to get as much of it as you can! But there's also the priceless education that comes from learning from the lessons in your life.

I am reminding myself to replace "why is this happening to me" with "what am I supposed to learn from this?" Learn from your mistakes, your victories, your failures, and your successes.

Get busy making the most of what you have, and if what you're doing isn't working, try something else.

Love Or Control?

A couple of years ago, I dated a gentleman who was very much in love with me, and he told me so just 5 weeks into our relationship.

I felt very pressured to return his feelings, even though the relationship was still new.

Over the next few months, I spoke to him no less than 3 times about how I felt that he was rushing things emotionally, which made me feel pressured.

I felt as if he already had a wedding dress, he just needed a girl to fit into it!

He was so focused on making his dream of a relationship into a reality that he didn't seem to be getting to know ME – he just wanted to fast-forward to his ideal marriage. (By the way – a lot of men feel this is what women do to them when dating!)

I was trying to give myself time for my feelings to develop, but they never did. Perhaps because of the constant pressure, but possibly because I just didn't feel the right chemistry with him.

Meanwhile, there were several red flags popping up, but I was justifying them as being the result of his love for me.

For example, he would pout when I would plan trips to the West Coast to see my family. He would argue with me when I wanted to end dates earlier than he did. He would whine when I wanted to cancel a date when I wasn't feeling well and wanted to rest. T he bottom line was, he wanted me to do what he wanted me to do.

When I asked for a few days of space so I could think about whether or not I wanted to continue the relationship, he blew up my phone; alternately begging, encouraging, and accusing me.

Needless to say, I ended the relationship.

It's completely normal and healthy to want things to go a certain way in life. However, when you're dealing with other people, you can't control the outcome!

If you're dating someone and he would rather spend the weekend with his friends than with you, it's because he'd rather spend the weekend with his friends than with you!

One truly great thing about men is that they do what they want!

You can try to manipulate and get him to choose you, but that isn't "love," it's control. And, as someone who's been on the receiving end of it, it's not loving. I didn't feel respected and loved by the man I dated; I felt manipulated and controlled, which made me feel resentful.

This applies to ALL relationships: friends, family, coworkers. If your colleagues don't invite you to lunch, it's because they don't want to have lunch with you.

Is it possible that they think you're unavailable? Yes. If you want to be sure, invite THEM to lunch and see what happens. If they decline the invitation and don't invite you next time, let them go enjoy their lunch without you.

Does that hurt? It might. But it doesn't feel as bad as being with someone who resents you (if you've never had that experience, think of a 15-year old who is rolling her eyes and sucking her teeth at you every 5 minutes).

If you really love someone, you have to give them the freedom to make their own choices.

Now, you don't have to stick around...if your beloved makes a choice that hurts you or your union, you can choose to leave the relationship.

But you're not going to control people into loving you – not if you want real love. Real love is love that is born of freedom and choice – not coercion and manipulation.

There's usually one reason people don't spend time with you: THEY DON'T WANT TO.

Most of us, ultimately, do what we want to do. I claim to be too busy to call my friends, but I have plenty of time for Facebook and the Real Housewives of Everywhere.

If you'll back off the pressure and let people make their own choices, you may find that they'll choose you because they want to.

One of my girlfriends told me she'd given up on a guy when he started texting her again. She ignored him because she'd already had her feelings hurt by him, and because she was no longer trying to make things work, he suddenly found her attractive. No kidding! She was now relaxed and spending time with her was something he wanted to do, not something she was demanding.

When we demand that people include us, they don't want to. That doesn't always feel good. But it feels a lot worse to force yourself into someone's life and constantly feel that they resent your presence.

It's much more One-Derful to release other people and give them the freedom to do what they want. You may find that in doing this, you actually attract more of what you want. And that's a pretty One-Derful Life!

Not a Mother

When you're single with no children, Mother's Day can be a source of sadness. You go to church to find comfort, and all the moms are wearing corsages and the pastor preaches his sermon on what a blessing it is to be a mother. Ouch.

It's natural to feel left out and left behind. Especially when all your friends who are mothers tell you to enjoy your freedom and that, "It'll happen if you believe. Just have faith." It's hard to have faith if you haven't even had a date in 2 years!

But what's a true "mother?" Is it only someone who gives birth?

That can't be true because women who have adopted children are mothers, even if there is no biological relation.

And, there are certainly women who give birth to and raise a child who do more harm than good.

Maybe it's a little easier for me because I made peace with my decision to not have a baby by myself, so I feel less sorrow about my "non-mother" status.

But I still feel left out – especially in a town where marriage and family are important social markers.

I used to have a lot of fear about my lack of children. And a lot of fear about the fact that I was okay with not having them.

One of my friends told me people who don't want children are mentally ill. That made me very anxious about my lack of maternal desire!

In fact, at one point, I was feeling that I should have children in my life. None of my friends had kids at that point, so I volunteered at the local children's hospital. That is a very intense experience and I highly recommend it to anyone as a terrific way to get your mind off your own problems.

I found that I didn't so much enjoy the company of small children, as I enjoyed helping and interacting with the exhausted, worried parents.

That was when I started to see that I have a lot of "mothering" qualities, they just express themselves in other ways.

Everyone on the planet has the opportunity to nurture, feed, provide for, care for, and love others.

It is true that I don't have any children. If I wanted kids in my life, I would have to find other ways to have them.

For example, babysitting for friends, volunteering at a school, helping out at Boys & Girls Clubs or a sports league or an extracurricular activity.

One could teach Sunday School or keep the church nursery or help out at Vacation Bible School. Singles can also be foster parents (I checked on that!).

Some women tell me they want their own children, not to watch someone else's. That makes me think of Romans 9:20-22. "But who are you, O man, to talk back to God? Shall what is formed say to him who formed it, 'why did you make me like this?'" (NIV)

I like the translation in The Message: "Who in the world do you think you are to second-guess God? Do you for one moment suppose any of us knows enough to call God into question?" Yikes.

I don't know why you don't have children. Maybe you're single and don't want to be alone to have children. Maybe you're like me and having kids wasn't enough of a driver to make you marry someone you weren't truly in love with.

Maybe you're married and your husband doesn't want them, or you both want them but are unable to conceive. These are all heartbreaking in their own ways.

I'm not saying that God is keeping you from having children, but if the reality is that you DON'T have them, you have to work within your current reality.

Like my favorite line from the movie "Shawshank Redemption": you gotta get busy living, or get busy dying.

You are a mother right now, whether you know it or not. Here's how:

Maybe you're a teacher (classroom, Sunday School, church nursery) and responsible for nurturing the minds and hearts of children.

Managing people at work. Doesn't it feel like your staff really is a bunch of 5-year olds sometimes?

Leading and managing involves nurturing people in that you have to guide them, praise them, and sometimes bring correction.

Mentoring people who are new in the faith or helping your friends through hard times.

Mentoring (even informally) a new employee on the job – taking him or her under your wing and helping them "learn the ropes."

Sometimes we want to be mothers because we want to love and be loved, but there are a lot of people around you who want to be loved!

I don't have a husband and children to cook for, so I have time to cook for sick or bereaved friends. I look out for my other single friends. I make myself available to talk with people who need help and guidance – that's what I would do for my kids if I had them.

And don't be so quick to avoid dating someone who already has children.

One of my male friends won't date anyone who already has kids, but he's in his 40's and most women in his dating pool do have children.

Be open to the joys of being a stepmother. Popular culture wants to paint a negative picture of the relationship between kids and a stepparent, but that stereotype doesn't necessarily reflect reality.

I had a very close relationship with my stepmom and had committed several years ago that I would always take care of her if my Dad ever passed before she did. Her death left a tremendous void in my life even though I was an adult and out of the house when she and my Dad married.

She never "raised" me, but she provided a lot of encouragement and support to me in my adult years – she was very much a mother to me.

In fact, one year she sent me a bouquet of flowers for Mother's Day from my dog because she was worried that I might feel left out on Mother's Day.

Remember that a lot of people around you need encouragement, support, guidance, nurturing and love.

They may not be an infant or a wide-eyed toddler, but everybody needs to feel loved and cared for.

Be open to God's ability to use you to nurture others. Maybe they won't be babies, but they still could use a "mother's" touch.

Don't pout and question why God hasn't blessed you with children. Get busy blessing the people around you. Feed them, send flowers to them, nurture their hearts and minds.

Be a mom now and then if you ever have children, you will have already had some practice!

Four Things Scarier Than Being Single

When I was in my early 30's, my greatest fear was being single in my 40's. Well, I'm in my 40's, single, and now I only fear two things: skinny jeans and the bathroom scale.

Folks, there are a lot of things that are scarier than "ending up" single. For example:

Being in a relationship where you are devalued. What does "devalued" mean? Any relationship where you are made to feel "less than" or your feelings, thoughts, and needs are disrespected and discounted.

The girlfriend who repeatedly says she'll meet you for lunch, then repeatedly bails at the last minute.

The guy you're dating who says he'll call you tonight at 7, then you don't hear from him for two days (and he wonders why YOU haven't called HIM).

The coworker who makes you the butt of her jokes during staff meetings.

These are relationships where you are being devalued. I recognize the signs of being devalued because for many years, I settled for relationships where I was devalued.

Why? Because I didn't believe I could do better. (I mean, "a bird in the hand is worth more than two in the bush," so a boyfriend who made me feel ignored was better than being alone, right? Wrong!)

Second, being in a relationship where you are the Consolation Prize.

Being the Consolation Prize makes you feel like you're wanted (kind of), but eventually you'll see that you're being settled for because the one he really wants isn't available.

You think you can upgrade to First Prize by being supportive and "better than" the Real First Prize, but you'll never be able to move up because Real First Prize is always there and IT'S NOT YOU.

I dated a man once who talked incessantly about his ex-wife and how terrible she was. He told me he loved me because I was so different from her. I thought I was "winning" because he would compare us and I seemed to come out ahead.

The key was, he was talking about HER. People talk about what they're thinking about. He was thinking about her. So much so, that he dumped me to go back to her!

If you've ever caught your man staring wistfully at an ex's photo, remembering good times with her, or talking about her (even negatively!) in excess, you know the feeling of the Consolation Prize.

It hurts because there's always a reminder that you're not really what he wants, but he'll settle for you.

Third (speaking of settling) - settling for someone for whom YOU don't have feelings.

This is reverse of BEING the Consolation Prize. In this scenario, you are making someone else your Consolation Prize, and it is almost as miserable as being settled for.

I've watched a lot of friends settle for men that are great fathers, but for whom they have no feelings of passion or excitement.

You can make that choice. Personally, when I have been in relationships with men for whom I felt no chemistry, I have been miserable, resentful, bored, and irritable – which inevitably leads to hurt feelings on both sides.

When you're in a relationship that "should be" what you want, but you find yourself envious of others in relationships that seem to have passion and chemistry, you may have settled. I'm not talking about how you started out 35 years ago crazy about each other and have settled into the routine, I'm talking about the guy you've been seeing for less than 6 months for whom you have no excitement.

When I'm perfectly content to see my "boyfriend" once a week, and I'm fine if he cancels plans, that's usually a clue that I'm settling.

Fourth, playing a supporting role in someone else's drama. If you find yourself constantly bailing your loved ones out of all sorts of jams – physical, mental, emotional, financial – you are on THEIR stage, not your own.

As women, we think it is loving and right to support our friends and family and "be there" for them. That's fine, if there's a give-and-take (or if the loved ones in question are minor children whom you are claiming as dependents on your taxes).

I recall the guy I dated who was always in the middle of some kind of drama: problems at work, problems with his ex-girlfriend, problems his ex-girlfriend was having in HER life that had nothing to do with him, problems with his ex-wife, problems with his grown children.

It was all about him, all the time. In order for me to support him, I had to abandon my work, my goals, and myself. I was focused on him; he was focused on him; and that left nobody focused on me – especially ME, who is the one person who should be focusing on me!

The good news is, you can avoid or exit these scary situations! And, if they come into your life again, you'll be able to resist them because you'll already know how bad they're going to make you feel.

Get Your Emotional Life Cleaned Up

My sweet sister-in-law uses a term that has stuck with me: being "emotionally clean." Used in a sentence: "It seems like you're in a clean place with this stuff with your friend."

I've been making powerful strides forward in my emotional life because I am committed to handling my emotional business "cleanly."

To be sure, I wasn't always clear on this, and spent many years handling things messily, thus creating even more emotional messes that needed to be cleaned up.

Our culture is very conducive to emotional messiness. Texting, social media, and gossip all support emotional messiness by allowing us to disconnect from our feelings and from other people and hide behind screens and erroneous "social proof." (If everyone is saying it, it must be true, right?)

It's much easier to break up a relationship via text or criticize someone on social media or talk behind someone's back about how she hurt your feelings – you don't have to face the person and be vulnerable and honest.

Why should you even care about emotional cleanliness? Well, how do you want to FEEL?

If you enjoy feeling hurt, anxious, misunderstood, and upset – emotional messiness is for you!

But, if you want to feel peaceful, in-control of your emotions, understood, and clear – you have to learn how to handle your emotional business cleanly.

Here's what I've learned about emotional cleanliness:

First, you have to get clear about what you're feeling.

You may talk to a trusted friend or your therapist, but at some point you are going to have to spend some time alone, quietly, to feel what you're feeling and then label it.

That's right: you have to say (to yourself FIRST) what I feel is _____ (sad, angry, hurt, scared, anxious, disappointed).

This may take minutes, hours, or days (or longer). "I feel like you can't be trusted," is not a feeling. "I feel hurt," is a feeling.

It took me a long time to be able to even identify any of my feelings because I spent years being emotionally shut-down.

I would feel sad, but would tell myself, "It doesn't matter – I'll be fine." Even, "I'm not sad, I'm just tired." And then I would work some more to avoid feeling sad so that I could have evidence that I was actually tired.

Second, you have to take responsibility for YOUR PART in your feelings.

In Twelve Step recovery, people learn to identify what they did to contribute to their own resentments.

For example, if your mother consistently makes jokes at your expense at family functions, you are participating in that by allowing the behavior and not setting boundaries and enforcing consequences.

You cannot control your mother's behavior, but you can stand up for yourself in a loving way.

If a bully were abusing your child in front of you, wouldn't you stand up for your kid? Do that for yourself!

Third, you must either choose to allow the situation to continue and be at peace with it, or you must change the situation.

Most of the time, the former is not going to work unless you're dealing with an aging parent with dementia or a special-needs child.

So, let's assume you have to handle something cleanly:

You will have to have a conversation with the person. Not a text-fest. Not a snarky social media exchange. Not taking it to a third party, unless you have both agreed to formal or informal mediation.

Here's the key: you have to be able to speak your truth without expectation of an outcome. You have to speak in a loving way, and you have to stay calm.

This is hard. I had to clean up 40+ years of emotional mess with some people.

Previously, I tried to have conversations about relationships that resulted in LOTS of hurt feelings on both sides.

With some of these folks, it took me a solid year to clean up "my side of the street" (as they say in Alcoholics Anonymous).

I got to a place where I could understand the other person's perspective and I was at peace with the fact that they were not going to change.

I also was clear about what I was and was not willing to do moving forward.

In one instance, the person called me and made some very unkind statements, which opened the door for a conversation.

Because I had done my work on my stuff, I was able to calmly and lovingly talk with them about my perspective on our relationship and how we had arrived there.

I also listened to their perspective and validated that I understood why they felt that way.

I took responsibility for my past behaviors, but I didn't expect an apology from them (which is good, because I didn't get one).

We both left the conversation with a better understanding of each other and some new agreements on how we will move forward.

When I hung up the phone, I felt healed rather than upset, and my interactions with that individual have been much more loving and positive.

Is this approach easy? No. It's not easy for a hoarder to clean up her home. Likewise, it's not easy to clean up emotionally, but if you want to FEEL better in your life, you have to do it!

I can testify that it feels One-Derful to be able to live in an emotionally clean space. I still have a way to go, but I'm focusing on "progress, not perfection."

Celebrate the Lesson

"I don't mind making mistakes, I just want to make new mistakes."

I heard that recently, and I love it! Sometimes we think that as we grow older, we automatically grow wiser, but I believe we only develop wisdom if we apply what we learn to our lives.

Wisdom won't always prevent us from making mistakes, but it will prevent us from making the SAME mistakes we've already made.

Honestly, one of the phrases I absolutely hate is, "everything happens for a reason."

Don't ever say that to someone whose child has died or who has lost a spouse suddenly or who has been the victim of a violent crime.

Here's the "reason" things happen: we live in a world where bad things happen to people who don't "deserve" them.

Maybe I'm splitting hairs, but I do believe in looking for the lesson.

Rather than saying "everything happens for a reason," which is very difficult to accept in the midst of a painful trial, I've learned to ask, "what is this here to teach me?" I believe we can learn from anything that happens in our lives.

And, in case you think the lesson is for you to learn how to suffer, that is incorrect. God doesn't benefit from you suffering (neither do the people around you).

Recently I was dating someone that I was very excited about, but it didn't work out. Was I disappointed? Yes. But rather than focusing on the feelings of disappointment, I am choosing to focus on the lesson; in this case, the lesson is that I can trust my intuition.

How will I use this lesson moving forward? When I get that little check in my spirit that "something ain't right here," I will listen to it rather than proceed forward. This will save me time and hurt feelings in the future.

Everybody in this life will suffer. In case you just thought about someone you envy who seems to "have it all," or everything always goes her way: yes, even SHE will suffer. She may be suffering now and you don't know about it. She may have suffered in the past. If not (and even if so), she will suffer in the future. We all do.

When you look back on the difficult times, what did you learn from them? NO! Not how to be miserable, broke, alone, and disillusioned!

If you honestly cannot find a valuable lesson in your experiences, you are moving in the direction of becoming the person Proverbs calls "a fool."

And, don't allow your lessons to be, "I learned never to trust anyone," "I learned all men are liars" (they're not), or "I learned that life is unfair." Come on! How miserable do you want to be?

I'm not saying you will see the lesson immediately. It's taken me years to learn the lessons from some of my life's most painful events. That's where your own perseverance comes in: you have to keep looking for the lesson.

You must continue to ask, "what is this here to teach me?"

If you cannot see the lesson, the Universe will keep sending you tests until you pass. You don't have to get an A, but you do have to pass the class!

If you cannot learn the lesson, you will keep taking the test. I signed up for Dating D-Bags 101 and had to take several tests before I learned the lesson: don't jump in quickly! Get to know the person and give it time to unfold slowly so you can see who you're dealing with.

I've also taken Breakup with Best Friend 215. In that course, I learned the importance of not talking about problems in the friendship with people other than the friend I'm having the problem with.

Fortunately, I was able to graduate to a new course: Reconciled with Best Friend 220.

If you want a One-Derful Life, you must see and hold on to the lessons in your experiences. You're going to make mistakes in life, but strive to make NEW mistakes. Learn from your lessons – that is where the blessing is.

It's My Time

I have to say that one of the things I really love about being single is that, for the most part, I get to spend my time however I choose to.

I know a lot of single folks feel lonely, and I do, too, at times – that is perfectly normal.

Sometimes singles romanticize "how much better life would be" if only they had "someone to share it with."

Most of the time, however, you are imagining what it would be like to have that special someone plugged into your life, and you forget that you would have to plug into his (or hers – I know you're reading, guys!).

"That's ok," you say. "I would love to participate in my fella's life." That's because you imagine an exciting Prince Charming who will whisk you off for exciting and glamorous adventures.

The last guy I was in love with is a great example. I so wanted to a part of his life, and I wanted him to feel for me what I felt for him (he didn't).

So I said "yes" every time he asked me to do something. But we never really did anything that I liked.

For example: spending an entire day repairing a mobile home as part of my boyfriend's pet charity project.

Or eating his grandmother's gut-wrenching casserole, then being stuck watching NASCAR with his uncle because my guy had fallen asleep on the couch.

Then there was painting his living room.

One time I thought we were going to have a fun weekend at the beach, but all we did was sit around his aunt's house and listen to her screaming children.

He did take me to a dive bar to get a bite to eat that weekend. That's right – one meal "out on the town" in an entire weekend at the beach.

Some girls might find a lot of pleasure in those activities; I don't.

The reality is, life as a couple isn't always an exciting adventure that could be the basis of a TV miniseries.

In fact, most of the married women I know have very little time available to themselves (especially if they have children).

There are some really great advantages to being single when it comes to how you spend your time.

You can decide with whom you are going to hang out. You get to choose which friends you have dinner with, go to the movies with, and attend parties with. You can also opt to not hang out with anyone!

Maybe you need a night by yourself with 4 boxes of Girl Scout cookies and Seasons 2 through 10 of "Grey's Anatomy" (don't judge me).

You can chat with friends or family on the phone for as long as you like without anyone else making snide remarks or overhearing you.

By the same token, you can turn your phone off if you need some quiet time (or if you just find it hard to carry on a conversation while inhaling an entire box of Thin Mints).

You can spend as much time as you want cleaning your house, and nobody will come along 10 minutes later and mess it back up (unless you have children or a mischievous puppy).

You are free to accept or decline invitations as you like. Many of my married friends have to skip fun events because they have to attend their husband's boss' party or they just feel guilty asking him to babysit after a long day so they can have "girls night out."

You can sleep in. Or, you can get up early and go the gym. You don't have to cook dinner, unless you want to.

I love my mornings as a single person. I get up early and workout. Then I spend about 45 minutes (sometimes more, sometimes less) drinking my tea while writing in my journal and having my morning meditation & prayer time. I make the bed and clean up the breakfast dishes because I like coming home to an ordered house – not always the case when you have a hubby!

Actually, I love my evenings, too. I am free to attend events as I see fit – sometimes I have an event at work that I need (or want) to attend, or a party I'd like to swing by.

I can also accept last-minute dinner invites from my gal pals.

I can go to bed at 9 o'clock without anyone teasing me.

If you are in a relationship, sometimes the other person's schedule dictates what you can do and when you can do it.

I dated a guy for a while who was an avid deer hunter. I spent a lot of evenings alone because he would rather sit in a deer stand than take me out to dinner. Actually, that's kind of hurtful now that I think about it.

When you're single, you can pursue interests and hobbies that you frequently let fall by the wayside when you're in a relationship.

You can enroll in a class or attend a Bible study. You can go to church wherever you want to go (or skip when you want to skip). You are free to help others. You can carry a meal to a grieving family or drive a sick friend to the emergency room.

Your One-Derful Life means you can spend your time the way you want to. Enjoy it - that is one of the things that will change if you get into a relationship.

Are You Part of the Problem or Part of the Solution?

I recently heard an interesting idea – not necessarily a new concept, but a timely application of something I'd heard before.

I was listening to a podcast and the host was talking about GMO's (genetically modified organisms) and eating organic foods. Her statement was that she cannot single-handedly run large, corporate farms out of business, but she doesn't have to support them with her dollars. She doesn't have to participate in their system.

With respect to food, I agree with her. I've been reading a lot about our food supply, GMO's, and the value of organic foods.

(If you want a startling education about food in America, read *The Food Revolution* by John Robbins.)

I feel very discouraged and frightened by what large corporations are doing to our food, and there is no way for me as an individual to change what is happening at the hands of the government and these corporate titans.

However, I can choose not to participate. I buy certified non-GMO and certified organic foods whenever possible.

I buy wild-caught fish rather than farmed fish.

In 1994, I began eating a vegetarian diet – partly because of the concerns I had about hormones and antibiotics in our chicken, beef, and animal-based products.

In 2001, I reintroduced fish into my diet, but I still avoid chicken and beef. I'm not a vegan, but I do eat certified organic dairy and eggs to protect myself from hormones and antibiotics.

I'm not interested in controlling or influencing what others do; I'm just making a decision not to participate in the drugging and mistreatment of the cows and chickens we use for food.

Also, I don't want antibiotics and growth hormones in my body.

I've been applying this idea in other areas of my life, too.

I was dating a fellow recently, and asked him for a few days of space to think about the relationship and what I wanted.

He was unable to give me space, and proceeded to blow up my phone with calls, voice mails, and text messages.

I realized that even though he was unable to respect my request for a break, I could respect my own request.

So, I ignored his texts and calls for the three days I needed to get clarity.

After I ended the relationship, I "blocked" him on my phone so I don't receive any calls or texts from him. Again: I am choosing not to participate in the drama.

I can choose to respect my own boundaries, even if someone else isn't.

I've heard it said that you're either part of the problem or part of the solution. When you participate, even passively, in a problem, you are furthering the problem.

As a teacher, I cannot allow a chatty student to hijack my class. If I don't confront the disruptive behavior, it will continue and escalate – it never gets better on its own! I have to solve the problem by correcting the student's behavior.

I had a friend who was involved in some very self-destructive and reckless behavior. I preached, I listened, I begged, I pleaded, I supported, I suggested; I did everything I could to "save" him from his bad decisions.

Sadly, all of my advice seemed to fall on deaf ears. Even more sadly, I was spending a lot of my mental and emotional energy on his life, until I was so burned out that I had to end the friendship to save myself.

I could no longer participate in his manufactured drama on any level because not only was my participation not helping him, it was harming me.

The One-Derful thing about deciding not to participate in something, is that you don't have to make a big deal about it – you can just quietly stop participating.

There's an organization in town that I have a very low opinion of. I don't publicize my negative experiences with the group, but I don't support any of their causes or events. I don't discourage others from participating, but I choose to spend my time and money elsewhere. There's no drama surrounding it – I just quietly decline invitations to their activities.

My life is becoming more One-Derful as I make these decisions about where to participate.

When I stop being part of the problem, I open up space in my life for new blessings. I'm less stressed, and I'm more available for healthy experiences.

From Bitter to Better

My brother once said something to me that has become my One-Derful Life mantra. He was frustrated with my, "I wish I could find someone" routine that frequently morphed into "my life is worthless because I'm alone."

He hit me square between the eyes with this: "If you're going to end up single, you'd better hurry up and make peace with it so you can enjoy the rest of your life."

I thought I had made my peace with being single, but I realized that giving up and acceptance are not the same thing.

I saw that I had a root of bitterness growing inside my spirit, and I don't want to be the bitter, angry woman who thinks her life is miserable because she's single.

A number of years ago, I was in a session with one of my spiritual mentors and she advised me that I "had to accept that I might remain single." I told her, I DON'T accept that – unacceptable – I want to be in a relationship.

She understood my desire, but she still told me I had to consider the possibility that I might not get what I want.

Again, I told her I WILL NOT accept the possibility that I would remain single.

Her response: "We can't do anything more as far as your spiritual growth and development if you're not even willing to consider the possibility."

So, I asked myself: what kind of life do I want to have?

I want peace, I want to feel secure (big driver in my search for a relationship – I want to feel like I belong somewhere), and I want to be able to enjoy life.

I believe those goals line up with the Bible, but God doesn't promise to deliver them in the way I think is best.

I believe God is more concerned with content than with form. In other words, I think He cares more about our attitude and heart condition than he does about the new car or boyfriend that WE think shapes our attitude and heart condition.

Nowhere in the Word does it say we are going to get everything we want. I am starting to believe what Paul said, "I have LEARNED to be content."

What kind of life do you want to have? Regardless of the circumstances, how do you want to feel as you move through life?

As long as your ability to have what you want is tied to people and situations, you will never be free to enjoy God's plan for your life.

My problem is, I don't know if I want God's plan (because I don't know what exactly what it is) – I want MY plan.

Unfortunately, MY plan doesn't go so well. Both could include me being single, but I believe if

I'm working God's plan, I have a better shot at enjoying my life.

So, I had to decide once and for all: who is going to be my god? God or me?

Actually, I've already had plenty of experience trying to run things my way – that got me a lot of heartache, consequences, anxiety, and hopelessness.

In Jeremiah, the Lord says, "I plan to give you hope in your future."

I cannot give myself hope because without God my future looks a lot like my past.

I never want to admit this, but I was mad at God because He wouldn't give me what I've been asking for.

Which, by the way, isn't abnormal or inappropriate – it's perfectly natural to want a relationship.

If I'm going to call myself a Believer, I have to believe. If I'm going to see ALL things work for MY GOOD, then I have to trust Him to work them out.

Trust always involves unanswered questions. But I would rather walk with God and get HIS plan, than go it alone.

For me, "making peace" with singleness is now a daily reminder to myself that God has a good plan FOR ME (not just for everybody else). It may not look the way I want it to look, but He will take care of me.

I may not understand why things don't go the way I want them to, but I can know that He will provide for me and shelter me regardless of the circumstances.

Today, I don't feel angry about being single. Sometimes I feel like I'm outside, looking in the windows at a fun party that I'm not invited to. Sometimes I feel a little bit sad, but He's taking me somewhere other than that party. I have to make the conscious decision to TRUST that His somewhere is what's best for me.

That daily surrender is the only way to remove that root of bitterness so I can enjoy MY One-Derful Life.

Free to Be FREE

I know a lot of singles wish to be married, or at least "coupled." Sometimes you feel left out, especially in you live in a family-oriented town.

I used to wish I could meet the "perfect" guy – or even the "perfect" best friend. This person would want to do everything together, but mostly everything that I wanted to do.

In reality, I learned that in relationships, you are sometimes asked to do things you DON'T want to do.

For the most part, I have learned to enjoy the single life. And, when I am dating someone, I frequently start to feel trapped.

I don't want to hang out with the same person 5 nights in a row, or eat his mom's Sunday dinner, or go to his nephew's kindergarten graduation.

I'm willing to make compromises, but I like my life.

I've had boyfriends who get jealous about my work schedule, gal pals, and even my gym time.

Some women want a man who is clingy and wants to spend every moment with them.

Personally, I like some space. And, as it turns out, I have not yet found the one "perfect" date or friend who wants to do EVERYTHING I want to do.

If you think about it, you don't want to do everything your guy or BFF wants to do, either.

Now, I'm not saying that married life or a relationship isn't a good thing – it can be a very real blessing; but, one of the things you have to trade away is a certain level of freedom and independence.

If you're going to have a successful relationship, you're not going to get your way 100% of the time. Maybe not even 50% of the time.

So, while you're single, enjoy your freedom! If you are trying to meet a "special someone", you'll be more attractive if you're happy and carefree, so you might as well enjoy where you're at. For example:

When you're single, you get to keep all your money and spend it however you like. I know we ladies like to dream of a Prince Charming who will swoop in and save you from all your bills.

However, every man I've ever talked to about this has told me his dream girl is not a debt-ridden overspender who wants to charge up his credit cards.

Also, once you're married, you need to be in agreement about money – this is the number one issue couples fight about, and you may not get to spend everything you want.

Conversely, if your husband is the spender, you may not be able to save and invest how you want.

I really enjoy being able to spend my money as I see fit.

Let's face it: most men don't understand why we need 17 pairs of black shoes.

One of my friends has to hide her purchases from her husband because he gets mad when she buys more clothes and shoes.

I never have to hide anything I buy, nor do I ever have to ask permission to get a housekeeper, manicure, massage, or earrings.

Another friend of mine wants to de-clutter her house, but her husband pitches a fit whenever she tries to get rid of anything.

I just cleaned out all of my closets and my garage and nobody stopped me when I hauled things to Goodwill or the dump.

My house is a lot more organized, and I don't have to worry about someone bringing me more stuff (except for the additional 7 pairs of black shoes I hope are in my future).

I recently went to Myrtle Beach for a 4-day vacation by myself, which absolutely shocked several of my friends. They could not believe I would go on a vacation alone.

Here's what I love about vacationing alone: I can do what I want, when I want.

Last year, I went to Atlanta for a long weekend to see my first Major League Baseball game. My team was in town to play the Braves, so I went to Atlanta, stayed in my favorite hotel, and went to Turner Field to see 2 games.

I watched baseball, shopped, laid out by the pool, took naps, and ate more sushi than any one person should be legally allowed to consume.

I also went to visit the church of one of my favorite TV evangelists and got to watch him live and in person after seeing him on TV for years. Very cool.

I've also learned that if I wait for someone else to want to go do things, I might miss out.

When I was in college in Reno, Nevada, the opera "La Boheme" was being performed by the local opera company. That is my favorite opera, and I dropped several hints to the gentleman I was dating.

Two weeks after the opera left town, he asked me if I wanted to go. To this day, I still have never seen "La Boheme" performed live. However, I have made it my motto not to miss out on anything because I "don't have someone to go with."

Don't worry about what people will think if you go somewhere by yourself.

In the town where I live, I go to the movies, the community theater, the symphony, various art and cultural events, church, shopping, basketball games, baseball games, concerts, and parties by myself. Actually, the only thing I don't feel comfortable doing alone is going to formal, black-tie galas. I'm old-fashioned in that respect, and I understand that today's culture says it's perfectly fine for a group of singles to go to a prom or formal gala as a group, but I just don't feel comfortable with that (of course, I don't wear white shoes, pants, or dresses before Memorial Day or after Labor Day – old-fashioned, I know).

The entire time I've lived here, nobody has ever made fun of me (not to my face, anyway) for going to the movies alone. Or anywhere else, either. I'd rather go to a college baseball game by myself than miss out because none of my friends like baseball. And I always see people I know and end up visiting with folks.

Maybe if you go do some things alone and enjoy your freedom, you might meet a new friend or a new boyfriend – you're more likely to be approached by a nice guy if you're not in an intimidating group of 4 girls.

Don't miss out on life by building a prison of solitude for yourself. What if you never meet Prince Charming? Do you really want to miss out on movies, concerts, and vacations just because you were afraid to go by yourself?

Put on your big girl britches and get out there and enjoy this big, fun world! What if you end up with someone who doesn't want to travel or go to the things you would like to go to? You'll still end up sitting on the couch and you won't be living your life.

Right now, while you have your freedom, get out there and enjoy life. Look for me – I'll probably be there (movies, concerts, events, vacations) on my own, so come grab a seat next to me and let the show begin!

Declare your independence from the fear of doing things alone and start being free to be FREE!

Blessing or Lesson: Discerning the Difference

I've heard it said, "When God wants to bless you, He sends a person into your life; when the enemy wants to mess you up, he sends a person into your life." If that's true, how do you know the difference?

First, one way that you CANNOT discern the difference between a blessing and a lesson is by your emotions.

While I am a fan of following your intuition, I'm talking about the emotions that make you tell all your friends that you "just know" the guy who stood behind you at Starbucks is your soulmate.

You have one date with someone and think God sent the person as your life partner.

Jeremiah 17:9 says, "The heart is deceitful above all things and beyond cure. Who can understand it?"

If I had a dollar for every time I believed the Lord had sent a particular man for my blessing, I'd be able to retire this year.

Do you need to feel butterflies for a relationship? I believe you do. Should you be excited about someone you're in a relationship with? Yes. Should you make decisions and commitments based on butterflies and excitement? Maybe not.

Another way you CANNOT discern the difference between a blessing and a lesson is by listening to your well-intentioned friends who are peddling the Disney version of romance, whereby Prince Charming suddenly shows up, lays eyes on you, and you ride off into the sunset together.

Many of my good friends, upon hearing I had a date, have exclaimed, "I feel like it's God!" Which was really encouraging, until it turned out that the guy was more of a dud than a stud.

It's embarrassing to have to tell people either God sent me a loser or they were wrong.

A third way you CANNOT discern the difference between a blessing and a lesson is by random "signs."

For example: he's from Tennessee, and then everywhere you look, you see Tennessee license plates, paraphernalia for the Vols or Titans, or headlines from Nashville.

Psychologically, what's happening is that you are primed and sensitive to references about Tennessee because that is now at the front of your mind.

It probably doesn't "mean something" that you both had broken arms in the 5th grade or that you both love pineapple on your pizza.

Again, you are more prone to see these similarities because you are excited about the person. That's cool and fun, just don't make a big decision or commitment based on these surface facts.

So, how can you tell the difference between a blessing and a lesson? TIME.

You have to give the relationship time to unfold so that you can see who you are dealing with, and they can see who you really are.

Throughout the Bible, God tells us to "wait on" Him.

A friend of mine recently rushed into a marriage with a man that she declared was "sent by God," and she's now contemplating filing for divorce.

If the relationship is "from God," what's the harm in taking 12-18 months to get to know the person?

As women, we can be swept off our feet by a beau who is gung-ho to get married right away.

Again, that Disney fairy tale of being whisked off by Prince Charming gets the best of us.

We're told that men are commitment-phobes (not true), so when a man is talking marriage on the second date, we think we've struck dating gold!

Warning: many men know that talking about marriage is an effective way to get into a woman's life (and bed).

Personally, my experience has been that men who are in a rush to get married are frequently trying to close the deal before you find out about the dealbreaker they're hiding from you.

By the time you find out about it, you're already legally bound and emotionally shackled.

Listen, I've been single a long time, and I'm ready for a relationship! However, I've had the experience of a guy showing up in my life, seemingly randomly, and thinking he was the great love I'd been waiting for.

After months of emotional abuse at his hands, I started to think God probably didn't want me to feel anxious and devalued on a daily basis. If I had let the relationship blossom over time – even 6 months – I would have saved myself a lot of heartache and bills for therapy.

And when I say, "time," that means consistently spending time together. Not talking on the phone or Skyping for a year; not "dating" long-distance where you see each other once a month.

Regular, consistent time together you so can see how the person acts in his or her day-to-day life.

If you're "dating" long-distance, it's going to take a lot longer for the shine to wear off enough for you to see the real person.

If it's "meant to be," what's the harm in taking time to see if the relationship is truly a blessing or if it's a lesson?

If you're feeling pressured to rush things, remember that Jesus never pressured people to join him. God doesn't pressure us...He beckons us, and He waits for us to turn to Him.

A Party of One is Still a Party

When my best friend wanted to throw me a party for my 35th birthday, my response was, "What's there to celebrate? I'm 35 and alone – there's nothing to be happy about." Whine much?

One thing that is very different about the South is that people here are very focused on marriage at a young age.

Having lived and traveled extensively in other parts of the country, I can tell you that the obsession with marriage before age 25 is almost uniquely Southern.

I spent 3 weeks straight on the West Coast recently and NOBODY asked me if I was married or if I had children.

Even if you don't live in a small, Southern town, I do want to address the panic that many single women (and men!) feel about getting older alone.

First, I know 22 year olds who are anxious because they're not engaged yet (to whom I want to say, get back to me when you're in your 40's, kid, and we can really talk about what anxiety is).

Second, I've met men and women in their 40's, 50's, and 60's who also are fearful about being single or single again due to death or divorce.

Unfortunately, being married doesn't necessarily eliminate fear of the future.

One of my girlfriends is married to a wonderful man, but they never had children. She recently confided to me that as she gets older and realizes she will most likely outlive her husband, she worries about "who will take care of me when I'm old."

I won't tell you not to be afraid or that the anxiety is unfounded. I have struggled with the thoughts of "what's going to happen to me."

My own stepmother worried about what would happen to her if my father had preceded her in death.

Even though I committed to her that I would take care of her as my own, she still had that nagging insecurity – maybe that I'd change my mind, or I wouldn't really follow through.

I do know that a lot of married people with children also have fears and anxiety about the future.

One of my friends buried both of her children and faces her senior years as a divorcee with no offspring. So even having a family doesn't guarantee you won't be alone at some point.

So far, this chapter is pretty depressing, I know. My greatest fear used to be that I would end up 40 and single.

Guess what happened? I turned 40 and I'm still single.

The surprising thing was that I'm happy in my singleness – I never imagined that would be true.

Part of that transformation for me was realizing I don't want children. I know a lot of people (especially women) struggle with this. If you are serious about wanting children, you may have to make some difficult decisions – like whether or not to adopt or give birth to a child as a single woman.

If that's not for you, maybe you could have children in your life by volunteering at a church, a hospital, or a children's charity.

There was a time when I really wanted to have children in my life so I volunteered at the local children's hospital.

Nothing will make you grateful for your life like spending time with ill children and their families. My point is, bloom where you're planted.

More importantly, God is not limited by your age.

I'm pretty sure this wasn't the scene in heaven when I turned 40: God slaps his hand over his forehead and exclaims, "You're 40?! Gee whiz - that really snuck up on me. Now what am I gonna do? Well, kid, I guess you're kinda screwed because you know how hard it is for a 40-year-old woman to meet a decent guy. Sorry about that. Wish there was something I could do for ya. How about a promotion at work, instead?"

In Isaiah 56:3-6, God says, "And let not any eunuch complain, "I am only a dry tree.""

Now, we don't encounter a lot of eunuchs today, but try this: "And let not any single person 35 or older complain, "I'm too old.""

I'm not saying you will "meet somebody." Maybe you will and maybe you won't.

There's a lot more to finding the right person than your age. But there's something way worse than being 35 and single – it's being 35 and miserable (whether you're single or married).

Single people think they'd be happier married, and a lot of married people believe they'd be happier single. We all do that.

My students think they'd be happier when they're graduated and working full-time, then they get out in the real world and realize they were happier in college!

God wants to give you a happy, abundant life worth celebrating at any age. Nowhere in the Bible does it say God's blessings are only for couples.

If marriage was the path to happiness and marriage, why was Jesus unmarried? Marriage wouldn't have kept him from being abandoned, forgotten, or forsaken.

You, on the other hand, are not abandoned, forgotten, or forsaken.

In Isaiah 56, God says if you bind yourself to Him, He will give you joy.

Maybe you can't really imagine that or believe it today, but I promise you that if you take your focus off your age and your marital status and focus on living a joyful life with what you have now, you will experience peace and happiness regardless of your circumstances.

Your future may not look like a fairy tale and it may not be what you had wished for, but it can be happy and joyous.

Is it possible that God can provide you with a better life than the one you imagine for yourself?

Here are some things worth celebrating about being single: you get to go see any movie you want to see with anyone you like without having to worry about anybody getting jealous. You can decorate your home as you see fit. You can leave your dirty laundry all over the place until you decide to pick it up. You can eat all the ice cream directly out of the tub with a spoon. You can drink out of the milk carton. You can buy 57 pairs of black pumps just because you like them. You don't have to shave your legs if you don't want to. You have freedom to do whatever you want to do. You can sleep in, get up early, lay on the couch all day, or shop 'til you drop.

If you can't get excited about celebrating your age because you're single, just celebrate your life. You are free, you are healthy, you are whole, and you have access to the Creator every day.

Let today be the day that you thank God for your One-Derful Life as it is now and ask Him to show you the life He has for you.

Then celebrate with another pair of shoes or another spoonful of ice cream.

Getting Balanced

I receive inspiration in a variety of places. Recently, in a yoga class, I was meditating on the need for balance in my life when I envisioned my life as a wheel. Maybe it's a pie, but that brings up my food issues, so I prefer to think of it as a wheel. A Wheel of Balance.

When I considered my life, I came up with eight distinct areas (in no particular order of importance because they are all equally important!): physical self care, service, home, learning, work, relationships, spiritual life, and fun.

I tend to get out of balance. I will focus obsessively on a friendship that is in trouble or I'll use work to escape.

Sometimes I make unwise decisions that undermine my physical health (mostly related to cupcakes, but that's a different story altogether).

Sometimes I forget to have fun! Sometimes I even forget what things I consider "fun!"

As I envisioned this Wheel of Balance, I answered the question posed by one of my yoga teachers: what is the one thing you absolutely cannot live without in this life (other than food, air, water).

For me, I cannot live a fulfilling life without a strong sense of peace. For me, my spiritual life is an important part of feeling peaceful.

Therefore, my relationship with God is at the center of my Wheel. Then each of the eight areas of my life holds an equal share of the remaining space.

Physical self care includes taking care of my body – getting enough rest, eating healthy food, exercising.

Service to the community and to other people is important to me.

Taking care of my home is on my Wheel because I want to have an ordered living space. My home is my sanctuary, so taking care of it matters.

I find it important to balance my thought life – learning new career skills, learning new ways of dealing with life – all part of my learning area on my Wheel.

Work includes my teaching and my business endeavors.

Relationships include family, friends, and other relationships.

Spiritual life for me includes my spiritual practice – prayer, meditation, reading spiritual Source material.

Fun includes activities that help me connect with myself – reading, traveling, attending events that I enjoy (I'm a nerd: I like the opera, the symphony, movies).

Thinking of my life in this way helps me to keep things in perspective. This way, if I'm upset over a conversation with a friend, I can see that my relationship with her is only part of one area – it's not even the entire relationship area!

Not that it doesn't matter, but it doesn't matter more than other parts of my life. This way, when life shifts and changes, I can maintain a sense of stability because I can see that if a client "fires" me, that's only part of one area of my life. It's not my identity, and it's not the only thing I have going on in my life.

My Wheel also helps me remember my blessings. Maybe a friendship ended, but I still have other relationships, and seven other areas of my life where I can see good things happening.

This helps me not fall apart when things appear to "fail" in my life. And, sometimes things leave and create space in an area for new experiences and people!

If I go through a season where there seems to be change in several areas of my life, I can always look at the center of the Wheel.

If I'm pursuing my relationship with God, I am grounded in the most important way. Also, if things aren't working in a lot of areas, I can look at that center piece as a way to make sure I'm putting first things first.

I like the Wheel because it reminds me that I do have a One-Derful Life! The Wheel is self-contained and isn't dependent on other people or on situations being exactly how I want them to be.

It also reminds me not to put people, work, or any other area at the center of my life – that place needs to be reserved for the Lord if I want my life to be balanced and to keep negativity at bay ("Be well balanced, be vigilant and cautious at all times; for that enemy of yours, the devil, roams around like a lion roaring in fierce hunger, seeking someone to seize upon and devour." 1 Peter 5:8).

Maybe this will inspire you to create your own Wheel of Balance and use it to map out YOUR One-Derful Life. It's a great reminder that you are complete within your own life!

5 ½ Rules of Singleness

I love structure and order.

I adore processes and systems.

I am infatuated with checklists and policies.

I know not everyone is as dependent on organization and labeling as I am, but structure helps me understand what to do, and order helps me feel safer and more peaceful.

As such, I present these "rules" to help make your single life easier to navigate, more pleasant, and less confusing.

Rule 1: Don't gripe about men. I know it's in vogue to complain about how horrible men are. Even married women do it – they bond over pinot grigio and stories about their lovably dense husbands.

But what you focus on grows. When you are complaining about men, the lack of men, or your negative interactions with men, you will see more to complain about.

Also, it's not attractive – meaning, you are not attracting to you what you want. If you want a man in your life, complaining about men does not make men want to spend time with you!

And, when your brain hears you being negative about men, it believes you and that reinforces your experience.

You become more strongly convinced that "men are _____ (fill in negative descriptor here)," and then it's a vicious cycle of complaining, having more to complain about, ad infinitum.

Rule 2: Don't hang out with married men. Unless their wives are with you. Call me old-fashioned, but it is not appropriate to spend time with someone else's husband.

I don't care if she said it was okay; I don't care if it's "just a cup of coffee."

Forming friendships with married men (apart from their wives) is a path to extramarital affairs because you open up to each other, he talks about his marriage, you're the supportive friend, then the feelings start developing.

If you don't want to waste time with unavailable men, don't spend time with men who are unavailable.

Be the fifth wheel, ask your friends to set you up with a single friend and double date, or sit home alone.

If you live in a small town, people WILL gossip about you when they see you out for coffee or a meal with a married man, even if it's a business lunch.

I'm speaking from experience here: your life becomes much more complicated when you are in a close friendship with a married man. You have no business hearing about his marriage or other intimate details of his life.

I recommend the book, *His Needs, Her Needs* by Willard Harley. It's about affair-proofing your marriage (married gals – read it NOW!), which doesn't apply if you're single, but it is valuable information while you're single and for your future relationships.

Rule 3: Do fun stuff. (Not with married men – see Rule 2). Don't sit at home because you "don't have anybody" to do things with.

There are times where singleness means you sit home alone or you go have fun alone.

If sitting home alone is your definition of fun, great. If not, go do what you want to do!

I routinely travel alone, dine alone, and go to sporting events, operas, symphonies, parties, and cultural events alone.

Nobody has ever made fun of me (to my face, anyway), and I usually end up meeting great folks.

You never know: maybe your soul mate is going to that baseball game and if you're there alone, he'll be able to approach you and start a conversation!

Rule 4: Don't waste time on men who don't have their lives together.

Time is your most precious commodity, and you can lose years waiting for a man to get it together.

This becomes more critical the older you get. If you're over 35, don't invest years with a man who has zero career direction (or ambition), lives with his parents or roommates, or is in bankruptcy.

If you're a do-it-yourself, love-a-project kind of gal, you may be attracted to that lovable guy who just needs a little "tweaking" (not to be confused with twerking) and he'll be "perfect."

Men don't change, and they especially don't change when a woman sets out to change them. Accept him how he is now, let him be free to go get his life together, and then he can find you when he's ready.

Rule 5: Take responsibility for where you are in your life. You are where you are because of the decisions and choices you have made up to this point.

I resented and resisted that idea for years, but the truth is: I'm not a victim.

I have chosen to hang onto dead-end relationships hoping they would make it.

I have chosen to involve myself with unavailable men.

I have chosen to rush into relationships with abusers, addicts, and losers only to find out what I was dealing with after I was emotionally invested.

I have chosen to live in a town where singleness is difficult.

I have chosen not to settle.

Stop blaming your ex-boyfriend, ex-best friend, ex-husband, parents, God, or the economy and be honest about your role in getting you where you are.

And a little add-on (that's the ½) – take responsibility for where you're going.

The good news is, you are not at anyone else's mercy when it comes to your life.

You're not a tree – you can move if you're unhappy.

There is a 100% probability that if you're reading this, you are not a slave (although you may feel like one). You can change careers, or start saying no to things you don't want to do.

Don't wait for Prince Charming to show up for you to get some direction! Get moving toward your goals – maybe Prince Charming is down the road a bit, and you'll meet him once you take a different path in life.

Even if you never meet him, you have to live the life God gave YOU.

These rules may seem a bit heavy-handed, but I promise they will lead you to a One-Derful Life.

Life Management 101

"Do you need more in your life, or do you need to be a better steward of what you already have?"

This is the question that recently hit me upside the head. I heard it during a presentation by one of my favorite teachers and authors; she was referring to financial issues, but I think the sentiment applies to any area of life.

Human nature is to look at what we don't have and think that if only we had that missing something, everything would be alright.

This author went on to say that happiness isn't about getting the best in life, it's about making the best out of life.

Singles think life would be better if they were married. Married people think life would be better with children. Parents think life will be better when the kids are older. Some people think life will be better if they were single instead of married to the person they are married to.

If you made more money, lived in a better house, drove a nicer car, had less family drama.

Everybody has some area in life that they wish would change. Just because they're not telling you about it, doesn't mean they aren't struggling with it.

But, if you think back, when you got the thing you wanted, you may have been satisfied for a time, but then you found some new unmet need that, "If only THIS were different, then I'd REALLY be happy."

Am I being a good manager of what I already have? In business, we teach students (beginning in the very first freshman business course) that there are 4 components to "management."

Those components are planning, organizing, leading & motivating, and controlling. (Before you get excited because you have the "controlling" thing mastered, "controlling" in this context refers to being able to see if what you're doing is producing the desired results, and making changes to produce different results. Not controlling other people, mind you. Controlling your own behavior and adjusting to the situation.)

All of these areas can apply to your everyday life.

Planning. Do you have a vision for your life?

My plan used to be very structured: married by age 35, Vice President of Marketing by 40, making six figures by 41.

Now I have a different plan – to be happy regardless of my marital status, job title, or net worth.

If nothing in your life changes, what is your plan to be happy?

I heard it this way, "God doesn't call us to be busy, He calls us to be fruitful."

Organized. Are you being a good steward of what you've already been given? If not, why would God give you more?

If you're not grateful now, you won't be grateful with more because the problem isn't the stuff or the circumstances in your life. If you're not grateful, the problem is in your mind and heart and spirit.

Paul said he had LEARNED to be content, whether in need or in abundance.

Leading & Motivating. If you know anything at all about people, you know that encouraging and supporting will do more to motivate others than criticizing and tearing down.

Do you lead and motivate YOURSELF? Most women have a negative self-dialogue in at least one area of their lives.

"I'm such a fat pig." "I hate my thighs." "I'll never find anybody." "I'm such an idiot." "I'm a loser." "My kids will never straighten up." "We can't afford that." "I'm tired." "I'm stressed." "I don't have time."

And we wonder why we're depressed, anxious, and miserable. You wouldn't say those things to someone you loved.

Would you tell your best friend that she's gained a lot of weight and looks like a big, fat pig? I hope not!

Would you tell your children they're losers? Would you tell your parents that they've wasted their lives?

If you want to start feeling better NOW, you must STOP the negative internal monologue.

I recently learned a great technique to help with this: the Rule of Opposite Thinking. Instead of "I'm a fat pig," choose "I am grateful to my body for everything it allows me to do."

If you really are dissatisfied with your weight, research shows that beating yourself up WILL

NOT motivate you – it will make you feel worse and will drive you right into a bag of donut holes. Choose the Opposite Thought: I am committed to taking good care of my body.

Controlling. Here's a simple question: do you have the results in your life that you want? If not, you need to make changes.

Some things you won't be able to change in terms of the circumstances or other people involved.

But the one thing you can always change is how you think about things.

What do you have to lose? If what you're doing up to this point isn't making your life better, you need to do things differently.

Waking up every day and hating your body, your job, your singleness, or any other part of your life is not getting you closer to the One-Derful Life you want.

What if things never change? Do you want to be miserable until you die? Of course not. We must LEARN to be grateful stewards of what we have now.

It's good to make changes and work towards a better life, but it's even more important to be grateful for NOW.

Remember: happiness doesn't come from things getting better, happiness comes when we make the best out of things. That's the key to the One-Derful Life.

Nurture Yourself

Mother's Day can bring up a variety of feelings, particularly if you are not a mother, or if you've lost your mother.

When we think of mothers, we think of nurturing, caretaking, and unconditional love.

Many times, mothers are so busy taking care of their children that they forget to take good care of themselves!

Maybe you're not a mother, or maybe you're a busy mom – either way, do you nurture yourself?

When I hear the word "nurture" I think about tenderness and loving support.

Do you nurture yourself? Are you tender and lovingly supportive of yourself in thought, word, and deed?

I think many of us are actually abusive towards ourselves.

A couple of years ago, I was going through a very difficult time and one of my girlfriends said I was a victim of emotional abuse. The abuser? Me.

My thoughts, words, and behavior towards myself were mean, disrespectful, and unloving.

Many of us have negative internal dialogues, use our mouths to speak unkindly about ourselves, and engage in behaviors that are unhealthy.

As Geneen Roth pointed out in *Women, Food and God*, we seem to think that if we punish ourselves, we'll end up more loving. If we are unkind to ourselves, we'll have more peace.

The truth is, the worse we treat ourselves, the worse we feel, and the worse we act – it's a vicious cycle of viciousness.

What would it look like to be nurturing towards oneself in thought, word, and deed?

First, your internal dialogue. What do you think about?

I have been more devoted to my meditation practice, and I've heard people say, "I just can't meditate – I don't know how."

If you can obsess over what your snarky sister said to you two years ago, or if you mentally rehearse the fight you'd like to have with your coworker, you know how to meditate.

We spend a lot of time thinking about negative things: what's wrong with us, what's wrong with the people we know, what's wrong with society, what's wrong with our workplace.

When you mentally pick on yourself by thinking about all of your mistakes, shortcomings, and "failures," you are not motivating yourself to do better.

We think that if we remind ourselves of our failures we will be inspired to do better.

However, every piece of research on this – from diets to management theories – shows us that repeated, negative reinforcement de-motivates people.

You get so discouraged that you figure, "hey, I'm such a screw-up I may as well eat the whole box of donuts."

Mental habits can be very difficult to break. It takes discipline to change your thinking, but St.

Paul said we could be "transformed by the entire renewing of [the] mind." (See Romans 12:2)

Perhaps you can wear a bracelet or a ring that every time you see it will remind you to think something positive or kind about yourself.

One of my spiritual mentors taught me to use a "switch word;" whenever I caught myself in a negative thought loop, I would say, "Thank you, God." That was a code to my brain to change my mental channel and think about what was going right.

Author James Altucher recommends thinking of 100 things you are grateful for. It's easy to come up with 10 or 15, but once you get around 37, you'll be really thinking about the good things in your life – even the small blessings!

It's hard to complain mentally when you're wracking your brain to come up with 100 things you're grateful for.

One of my good friends prefaces many of her comments with, "I know this is probably stupid, but...." Or, "I'm probably dumb for thinking this, but...." She holds a Ph.D. – "stupid" and "dumb" are not words that in any way apply to her!

I pointed this out to her as a way to help her break this habit. Don't use your own mouth to put yourself down! It is a physiological fact that your brain puts more weight on what it hears from YOU than anything it hears from anyone else.

If you are using your own voice to speak about yourself disrespectfully, your brain BELIEVES you! That's why, if you say you're ugly, even if the greatest guy on the planet says you're beautiful, you won't believe it (even if you want to).

Use your mouth to say nice things to yourself. Maybe not in front of other people (lest they think you have lost your marbles), but certainly don't speak ill of yourself in front of others! Stop putting yourself down!

If you have children (or if you would like to someday), would you keep them up all night, refuse to feed them nutritious food, deny them fresh air and water, and keep them from medical care? But we do those things to ourselves.

What would we say about a mother who was "too busy" working to take her child to the dentist?

And yet, we don't get the rest we need, the good nutrition we require, the fresh air and water that would rejuvenate us, and the regular medical attention that could help us prevent illness.

Part of feeling One-Derful is nurturing yourself. This isn't the equivalent of selfishness.

Nurturing yourself doesn't have to be "either/ or," it can be "both/and." You can nurture yourself and still take care of others. You are One-Derful! Treat yourself like the One-Derful creature you are!

Picking Up the Pieces

What do you do when things fall apart?

You know the feeling: you go through a time in your life where it seems like every time you turn around you're getting hit with a new crisis.

Right about the time you get one situation resolved, another one pops up. Sometimes the crises are major (end of a relationship, death of a loved one), but sometimes you're dealing with a series of small crises – either scenario can wear you down!

Before you know it, you're in the "what's next?" mindset – just waiting for the next piece of bad news.

Recently, I've been watching a friend of mine go through a tough time. Her relationship ended, but she immediately got into a new one. Her new guy is nice enough, but not emotionally available (in my opinion).

She hates her job and is threatening to quit, but doesn't have any other options (or even interviews) lined up.

She may move back in with her parents, but her mom told me that won't be an option. She's having financial problems, and is having trouble paying back the debts she's already accumulated.

A couple of us have tried to "talk some sense into" her, but to no avail. I can understand that – when I've been in the "life crisis" mode, you need help, but sometimes it feels like the help you're receiving is just criticism and drama.

Personally, when I'm in a place where everything seems to be falling apart, I fall back on what I call "the basics."

Whether it's health issues, heartbreak, career pressure, or relationship issues, I have found that I can weather the storm if I keep things simple.

First of all, don't make big decisions during a crisis. Obviously, you should decide to call 911 if the house is on fire, but don't break up with your boyfriend when you get fired from your job (unless you were dating your boss and he's the one that fired you).

It always amazes me how many students have "the talk" with their beloveds during final exam week. Wait until you've dealt with one crisis before you create another one.

Part of my thinking there is I believe in stopping the bleeding first. Don't create more problems by taking action because you're probably not in a great space to make wise decisions.

Stop, breathe, and don't take any major action steps until you're clear.

Speaking of clarity, this isn't a good time to medicate with food, alcohol, or other substances (even chocolate – sorry!). You need to give your body and your brain the space and clarity to get peaceful, which you can't do when you are hungover (either from food or alcohol).

In fact, this is the time to take care of yourself and give yourself the time and space to calm down and develop a healthy perspective. Get enough rest, eat healthfully, do yoga or get to the gym. I try to watch a little less TV and read one of my favorite books on spirituality.

Remember weight-loss sensation Susan Powter? "Stop the insanity!" Stop the crazy, lashing-out behavior. It's nobody else's fault that you're miserable. If it is, get away from that person. Otherwise, don't take your pain out on other people. It will create more problems, and you'll feel worse.

Being extra nice to people when I'm hurting helps me to feel better. Plaster a fake smile on your face long enough, and you will start to feel happy!

I believe when things fall apart, it's the Universe's way of pushing the reset button in our lives. Maybe God is trying to get your attention because you need to make some changes.

The only way to find out what those changes need to be is to get quiet and be in a place mentally and emotionally where you can hear the wisdom of Spirit.

The familiar saying, "if you keep doing what you're doing, you'll keep getting what you're getting" comes to mind. If things are falling apart, you may need to stop, wait, and listen for a new direction to go in.

I want my friend to stop, breathe, and get quiet long enough to receive divine guidance on the next step. Take it back to basics – chill out on the work drama, save some money, stop churning up more drama for herself.

Stop the insanity, girlfriend! That's the first step in putting the pieces back together in your One-Derful Life.

Man Up!

There are certain responsibilities a father has in a daughter's life: to provide, to protect, and to repair and maintain.

If your dad wasn't in your life growing up (or, if he was unable to meet these responsibilities), you may not have had a man to model what these behaviors look like.

However, if you are an adult, you are now responsible to yourself to do the job!

Many times as singles, we look to other people to provide for us, protect us, and "fix" us.

While I do believe that a man's role in a relationship is to cover and support his wife, that doesn't absolve her of her responsibility to take care of herself – and her husband!

Ladies, even though men do like to feel needed and they do enjoy helping and "fixing" things, no man is looking for a train wreck of a gal who is going to be more of a project than a partner.

Here's how to "man up" some areas of your life so that you will be the Good Thing your Boaz is looking for:

Provide. Please stop looking for a man to save you from your bills. You must provide for yourself.

Be like the Shulamite woman and have a "vineyard" that you bring (see "Song of Solomon").

The Proverbs 31 woman provided financially, spiritually, and emotionally for her household.

This doesn't mean that a man shouldn't provide for you, but don't expect him to rescue you out of a financial hole that he didn't dig!

You must be able to provide a good home for yourself before you can provide one for a family.

I'm amazed at the number of women who brag about not being able to cook or who are unwilling to clean.

I understand that when we work full time, it's hard to be a homemaking goddess. However, men value domestic support in the same way that women value financial support: it's how we can show each other that we're taking care of one another.

If you don't have the time or the energy to keep up your home, then hire someone to help you, or trade chores with a friend.

The husband of one of my girlfriends has grown exceedingly frustrated because my friend doesn't work full time; yet, the house is always a mess and "dinner" is usually a meal in a bucket or a bag from a drive-thru.

He'd prefer that she work full time and then they could use some of the extra income to pay for a housekeeper!

Protect. In the most practical sense, you do need to protect yourself from harm – physically and financially.

Don't put yourself in dangerous situations. Make sure you have adequate insurance for your possessions, life, and any injuries that you may sustain or cause.

You also have a responsibility to protect yourself mentally and emotionally.

Proverbs tells us to "guard your heart, because everything you do flows from it." (Proverbs 4:23 NIV)

You are man-repellant (and friend-repellant, promotion-repellant, etc.) when you are negative and bitter.

Be careful what you allow into your ears, eyes, mind, and emotions.

This isn't scientific, but my personal experience with people who watch a lot of horror movies (including the Home Invasion Sunday marathons on Lifetime) or who listen to too much talk radio or acid, death-metal music (or woman-bashing, authority-bashing rap) is that they tend to have a pretty negative outlook on life. There seems to be a lot of anxiety and depression there.

My mom and dad diligently monitored what I watched on TV, the movies I saw, and the books I read. Now, it's my responsibility to do that for myself because "everything I do in life" flows out of what's inside of me.

Repair and maintain. My dad is a man's man. He can fix anything. And if he can't fix it, he knows someone who can!

In the physical sense, it's good to have someone who can help you take care of the possessions you own.

However, when it comes to keeping YOU "fixed," this is a one-woman job!

I was on a date with a gentleman and when I asked him what he likes to do when he's not working, his response was, "Well, I pretty much just stay at home because I don't have anybody to do stuff with. I'm pretty bored."

Notice I asked what he LIKES to do – he could have dazzled me with things he would enjoy doing.

When I heard his response, all kind of warning bells went off in my head because if you're lonely and bored, then it's going to be MY job to entertain you...and I don't want that job!

There is only one person who is responsible for fixing your broken heart, repairing your attitude, alleviating your loneliness, and maintaining your sanity. That person is you.

It's great if a man in your life is available to fix your sink, but don't expect him to fix your soul.

Part of living a One-Derful Life that attracts other people is the ability to be whole, complete, and happy.

Get Real

I have struggled with anxiety for most of my life. It's normal to feel anxious for a "real" reason, like when you're waiting to see the doctor (right?), or waiting for test results, or about to speak in public (number one fear in America, by the way).

It's no fun to feel anxious during these times, but I think the most crippling type of anxiety is the fear of "what's going to happen" related to people and situations that may or may not be real.

Let me explain. Here are some of my favorite "may not be real" fears:

- What if my friend is mad at me? I don't know why she would be, but what if she is?
- What if people are talking about me and everybody in town ends up hating me?
- What if I lose my job and end up homeless?
- What if my boss wakes up tomorrow and decides he doesn't like me and I get fired?
- What if so-and-so doesn't want to be my friend anymore?
- What if my mom (dad, sibling, grandmother, 2nd cousin) is mad at me?

Some of my anxiety in these areas is because I have been friends with people (and dated men) who have suddenly, for no discernible reason, stopped speaking to me.

Mostly, however, these fears could be categorized as a "fear of others."

I think it's appropriate to fear another person if he or she is pointing a gun at you, but otherwise – being held hostage by these fears and anxieties is no way to live.

You feel insecure, you need constant reassurance that people aren't mad at you, and your entire well-being rests on feeling that everyone else is happy with you.

You may have heard the saying that "FEAR" stands for "False Evidence Appearing Real." I recently heard someone say, "I'd rather believe what I do know than what I don't know."

When you are making up scenarios and then living as if they are real, that is called "delusional."

In "The Secret Things of God," Dr. Henry Cloud proposes that successful people don't cower in fear if there is a problem – they confront it.

Certainly, there is a time, place, and a method of confrontation that is appropriate, depending on the situation.

I recently asked a friend of mine if there was a problem in our relationship. For the past year, I had been getting an uncomfortable feeling, and I had some actual examples (not just my own thoughts) to substantiate my concerns.

I didn't confront her because I was afraid, and I thought if she were upset with me, she would bring it up if she wanted to talk about it. But, after reading about healthy confrontation, I contacted her, asked her, and we had a very good talk.

I had, in fact, offended her, but she gave me the opportunity to apologize and we were able to set things right.

I have also used this technique at work. I don't recommend asking your boss if he or she is mad at you (you'll sound like a 10-year old), but if there is a legitimate situation that needs to be addressed, don't wait for the other person to do it – most people would rather talk behind your back (including, but not limited to, posting on social media) than talk to you calmly about what is upsetting them.

The key is, you have to be willing to listen, accept responsibility for your behavior, and make amends – which includes making changes in the future.

How do you deal with unfounded fears (like, "what if she's mad at me," or "what if....")? Pray.

I had an incident with a boss where a coworker had complained about me (making up a lie, by the way), and my boss was very irritated by the drama. I wanted to revisit the subject with my boss the next day, but I didn't want to bring it up because I knew the timing wasn't right. I prayed, but I made the decision not to approach my boss, even though that would make me feel better.

The next day, my boss called me in and touched on the subject, and I had my chance to say what I had wanted. It was well-received, and the problem was resolved (with me looking like the good guy).

Another time, I was afraid I had offended a dear friend's mother with an off-handed comment I'd made at a dinner party. I didn't want to ask my friend because I figured she didn't need the drama of a mother-versus-friend problem, and if I had offended her mother, she wouldn't want to be the one to have to tell me. It was so hard, but I prayed and waited, and recently, my friend volunteered that her mother was saying that she thinks very highly of me. Really? Whew.

I've been learning to discipline myself not to lose hours and days over anxieties that aren't real.

Pray, confront if that's appropriate, and don't let your mind spin endlessly around the "what if's."

You have to choose to think about something else – this is where discipline and self-control come in.

We're never going to get to a place where we don't feel fear or anxiety. But, I believe we can get to a place where those feelings don't have to rule over us.

If the same Spirit that raised Christ from the dead lives in you (per St. Paul), you are more than a conqueror. Jesus wasn't a victim, was He? Neither are you!

Conserve Your Energy

I once saw a television ad that captured my attention. The ad was about the merits of conserving energy; the basic message was, if you conserve energy, your power bill will be lower and you will have more money to spend on other things.

I liked the ad because I'd been thinking about energy drains – not of the drafty windows and light bulb types, but of the emotional and mental types.

I think energy drains exist in at least three areas: our physical environment, relationships, and mental processes.

Plugging these energy drains is important because, as my therapist taught me, your mental and emotional energy is like your bank account: it is finite, and you have to choose where to spend it.

Energy drains in your physical environment are the things that every time you see them, they irritate you.

One year, some of the fascia on the front of my house needed to be replaced. It was above the carport, so every time I left or came home, I saw two pieces of rotten wood and it irritated me. I felt like I wasn't being a good steward of the home I had. When I took the time to call someone to come repair it, I felt better.

Another example: permanently stained clothing or clothes that need to be mended.

You know the scenario: you're running late, pull out a blouse to wear, get it halfway buttoned and realize the last time you wore it, you popped a button off but didn't repair it. Now, you have to re-configure your ensemble for the day or sew on a button before work (like you have time for all that).

More common energy drains in your environment are clutter, old magazines or newspapers, and minor home repairs.

Sadly, it does take your time to plug these drains. And, it may take money. However, if you can't afford to pay someone to help you with home repairs, get creative. Maybe one of your friends will loan you her husband, and you can repay her by babysitting her kids.

If you have clothes that are stained or you're not willing to mend them, get rid of them.

Change the burned-out bulbs; throw away the dying plant; toss (recycle!) the unread papers and magazines. Tackle one drain at a time – you will be amazed at how much your aggravation level will decrease.

Relationships that are energy drains are those where you are giving, they are taking, and you've had enough.

Healthy relationships are give-and-take, not you-give-and-they-take-all-the-time. You know a relationship is draining you when you feel anxious when you know you will have to see the person, or you dread seeing their number pop up on your phone.

Recently, a friend of mine was telling me about a "frenemy" (friend/enemy) who was being incredibly insensitive and rude.

My friend's husband died very suddenly a few years ago, and she is still reeling from the loss. The frenemy had made some hurtful comments about widowhood.

My thought (and my advice to her) was, "you don't need the aggravation – avoid that person!" You already have enough grief; don't voluntarily sign up for more!

I have had to follow that advice. There are some relationships that you cannot take with you into a better future. You don't necessarily have to cut the person out of your life and have some dramatic falling-out, but you may have to change the form of the relationship.

For example, there may be someone you've been friends with for years, but the friendship no longer fits. Just like you may LOVE those pleated pants you wore 15 years ago, they don't fit anymore (they're definitely NOT flattering, and that's why they are out of style).

Maybe you have changed; maybe your friend has changed. Either way, if the relationship has become an energy drain, you have to move on because it's taking the energy you could use for work, dating, marriage, kids, or other friendships.

You're not expanding your well-being, you are shrinking.

If you want a better, more joyful future, you cannot take all of the people and situations from your present with you. Is that scary? Maybe. For me, the scarier option is staying miserable.

Mental energy drains are usually what we do to ourselves when we are worrying or obsessing about what happened, what is happening, and what is going to happen.

Another great piece of advice from my therapist: decide not to go down that mental road.

Or, decide that if you are going to think about your dating problems today, save worrying whether or not you'll get fired for another day.

This takes mental discipline. Many times we think, "I can't help what I think." Yes, you can.

I read once that His Holiness the Dalai Lama addressed worrying like this: "If there is something I can do about the situation, I do it. If there is nothing more I can do, what is the point of worrying? My worrying doesn't change the situation and it doesn't help me cope."

I love that! I find that when I am worrying or obsessing about what's going to happen, it is a symptom that I am trying to gain control over an uncontrollable situation. And, truly, my worrying doesn't impact the outcome, but it does make me more miserable and unable to enjoy the other things in my life.

Regardless of what you wish you could do, you cannot do everything. Your mental and emotional energy is limited. Spend it on the things that make your life better. There are a lot of energy drains you cannot control in your life (the economy, who you work with, traffic), so start plugging the ones you can plug so you can better cope with the uncontrollable drains.

Remember: if you want a different future, you have to change some of the things in your present.

Grow Up

We don't seem to have many people who can model what grown up, emotional maturity looks like.

Politicians duke it out on social media, calling people names, while journalists mock 15- year olds who survived a school shooting.

As reality TV continues to gain ratings, civility and emotional maturity seem to be fading away.

Part of being happy and living a One-Derful Life is walking in emotional maturity. Here are some thoughts on what that looks like:

Don't personalize. We tend to take things personally that aren't personal.

I used to think that my relationship failures were because God was punishing me. Turns out, the problem wasn't that God was punishing me, the problem was that I stayed in relationships that weren't going to work out.

The problem isn't even that I attract jerks - the problem is, I want to give them my phone number.

I've become a fan of Stoic philosophy, which basically teaches that events are neutral; it's our perspective that makes them positive or negative.

You're sad because your relationship ended, but three months later you read that your beloved was arrested for domestic violence.

You are upset over being fired, but weeks later your former employer is investigated by the IRS.

You think a raise is the key to your happiness, but then you see how much more you owe in taxes.

Part of being an emotional adult is recognizing that things happen. It's our response to those things that determines how they impact our lives. Maybe you can't control the event, but you can always control your response.

Take responsibility for your emotional state. Stuff is going to happen and people are going to do things.

I recently found out some information that really hurt my feelings. I agree with author Marianne Williamson: one of the words you can only truly understand once it happens to you is "betrayal."

When your boyfriend cheats on you or your colleague tells lies about you, you're going to be upset - no doubt about that. But, understand that you are a participant in anything that is happening in your life.

It takes discipline, but you have to take responsibility for where you are NOW and decide how you're going to proceed. Spoiler alert: venting on social media or sending a flurry of hateful texts may feel good in the moment, but it will end up causing you more problems. Every. Single. Time.

Instead:

Decide how you want to feel, then act accordingly.

For me, the most important emotion I want to feel is peace. More than anything, I want to feel peaceful.

I have learned that when something upsetting happens and my emotions are in an uproar, I need to figure out (fast) how to find a sense of peace.

That may mean apologizing, practicing forgiveness, praying for the person who betrayed me, or taking some other proactive step to help myself.

Again, venting on social media or sending those texts or emails may feel good in the moment, but I know it won't bring me peace.

Waiting for external conditions to make you feel good is a recipe for disaster - that is the definition of suffering: only being able to feel good when everything is how you want it to be.

I used to believe I could only feel truly happy and fulfilled if I had a husband and children. But, I'm still single, so I've had to figure out how to be happy and fulfilled because I may never have a family.

The cool thing is, once you get to that space of contentment, you really don't care about getting what you thought you wanted. Because you already have what you truly wanted all along: happiness and fulfillment.

Act calm. Listen, you're going to get upset - life deals us some pretty tough blows. It's perfectly normal to feel the feelings of anger, rage, sadness, depression, and all of the other difficult emotions.

You have a right to feel how you feel, but you don't have the right to act on those feelings - especially around other people.

Hopefully you have a trusted friend or a therapist or a support group to whom you can express your most raw and painful feelings.

I find journaling and prayer to also be lifelines.

But allowing your employees, children, students, or anyone who cannot get away from you to bear the brunt of your emotional storm is hurtful to them and damages your relationships.

Yes, you may be hoppin' mad at what your boss said to you, but your kids shouldn't hear you screaming about that.

People who depend on you (again: employees, students, children) need to feel that you are in control of yourself because they need to know you can create a safe environment. If they aren't safe from your emotions, they don't feel safe.

Part of being a grownup is you have to demonstrate maturity regardless of whether or not you "feel like it."

Do YOUR job. Your job is to deal with your own feelings. It is not someone else's responsibility to make you happy or keep you happy.

One of my girlfriends hasn't spoken to her brother-in-law for 25 years because, in her estimation, he still owes her an apology for something he said that offended her. Twenty-five years ago.

I can promise you, he doesn't even know she's still mad at him.

If you cannot move on until someone else does something, says something, or acknowledges something, you're going to be stuck.

Closure is overrated. Most of us think closure is when the other person understands our feelings; actually, closure is when you are able to express your feelings and move on.

And you don't have to express them to the person - sometimes that isn't a good idea! You can journal, talk to a friend, have an imaginary conversation with the person.

True closure does not depend on someone else's participation - you are the only one who needs to participate in order to get closure.

When we say we want closure, we normally mean we want the other person to say or do something to make us feel better.

If you're dating a guy and he ghosts on you (disappears), he's told you with his behavior that he's not into you. Do you really need to hear the words? There is nothing he is going to say that will make you feel better; in fact, anything he says will only (a) make you feel worse, or (b) give you false hope (which will eventually make you feel worse).

You don't need anyone to give you permission to close the door and move on.

Emotional maturity brings freedom. Freedom from feeling like you have no control in your life. Freedom from the drama you cause when you let your emotions run the show. Freedom to grow up into a person with more depth and substance as you learn to move through life with grace and poise. Freedom to live your own One-Derful Life.

What Are You Looking At?

I was in San Antonio, sitting on the balcony of my 4-star hotel room, overlooking the famed Riverwalk when it hit me: I'm living the life I dreamed of as a little girl. Well, mostly.

True, I dreamed I would be living this life as part of a couple, but a lot of the other parts of my dream are now my reality.

I have a career I love, I travel when I want to places I want (mostly), and I can shop pretty much anytime I want to.

So, if I mostly have my dream life, why am I not really excited about it?

That's when I realized I, like many people, am focused on what's missing rather than what's present.

As singles, we focus on the missing mate, but married people do this – everybody tends to focus on what they don't have, rather than what they do have.

This realization has caused me to commit to enjoying the life I have. The only thing that scares me more than being 60 and single is being 60 and miserable.

I don't want to waste days, weeks, months, and years unhappy because I don't have a man.

I meet a lot of single women and men who have decided they cannot be happy without a mate.

They say they're "fine," but their complaining, bitterness, and obsession with "finding someone" belies their deeply-rooted inability to enjoy life.

If you cannot be happy as a single, you won't be happy in a couple because YOU'RE AN UNHAPPY PERSON. Side note: unhappy people are not attractive.

I just spent several adventurous days in Boston. While there, I got together with a friend of mine who lives there.

A mere 20 mind-numbing minutes into our conversation, I could see he has decided he has to have a partner to be happy. Of course, he denied it, but his monologue went from whining about why women don't like him (hint: quit talking about your ex-girlfriend, The Stripper), to how people are worthless (thanks!), to how he's really doing great and enjoying being single (clue: this level of dishonesty is a red-flag to any sane woman whose job doesn't involve a pole).

One of my girlfriends has become so bitter over her singleness that she refuses to even go anywhere anymore. She hates seeing couples (I recommended she move away), she hates being reminded she's single, and she hates being alone.

I get it – it's the same feeling I have toward her when she starts that negativity!

What if you never get married? If you have decided you cannot be happy single, you may be in for many years of misery. People (men and women) pick up on that dissatisfaction, and it's very unattractive because you come across as desperate and needy.

Even if you do find someone, you will probably be unhappy because you're going to find out eventually that your partner cannot make you happy, keep you happy, or meet all of your expectations for happiness.

There has to be some area of your life that is going well that you can enjoy. If not, you're really not ready to meet anybody because you're a wreck and you need to get it together.

I asked my friend in Boston what he's looking for (other than another exotic dancer), and he wants a woman who's comfortable dressing up and going to black-tie events, who wants to jump out of airplanes, and who enjoys camping for weeks at a time. After all of that, she has to be wild in the bedroom and (my observation) able to listen to him talk about himself for hours on end.

I don't know if that gal exists anywhere on the Eastern Seaboard. Meanwhile, my friend is losing years off his life whining about how lonely he is.

Again, talking about your ex (exotic dancer or not) is dating repellant for men and women.

Get a therapist, get a life, get a prescription – do something to stop talking incessantly about your past heartaches! When you go on and on about The Last One, people know you're not emotionally available.

I hope I will have a family someday. We all want the same thing – to be loved, and to feel like we belong. If I ever have that, these are my single days and I want to enjoy them while they last! If I never have a family, I want to enjoy my single days because they may be here for a long time!

You can make this decision. You can decide to enjoy your life as a single person. How do you do this?

Stop telling yourself you can't be happy without a mate.

If you want to find the right person, you need to be the right person – maybe you need to make some changes.

Otherwise (and meanwhile), enjoy the people around you. Enjoy your surroundings. Enjoy the opportunities you have in your freedom.

I love opera, but it's an acquired taste, and I don't really expect that I'll find a guy who is excited to find "La Boheme" on an opera season schedule.

Even if I get married, I may still end up going to operas by myself. The probability that I will find a guy who likes going to basketball games, baseball games, symphony concerts, and opera is fairly slim.

One great benefit of singleness is that I can do all of that and not have to worry about someone pouting because I'm going out without him!

Regardless of today's date, decide right now that you are going to end this year enjoying your life. Believe me – I know that's a tough order.

Enjoy the One-Derful Life you have by being fully present and appreciating WHAT IS.

Tricks AND Treats

It's no treat when you feel like someone has tricked you.

We all know the feelings that come with being lied to, cheated on, stolen from, or betrayed in some way. Those feelings are numbness, sadness, disbelief, anger, anxiety, despair – just to name a few.

While it's virtually impossible to avoid being on the receiving end of such "tricks," I've been learning some methods for coping with the fallout.

First, look at your part. This is a concept that is foundational in most Twelve Step recovery programs.

The Fourth Step encourages participants to make a list of resentments, naming each offender and what he or she did to the participant. That part is always the easiest!

The more difficult task is to then identify what you did to contribute to the situation.

For example: I have a resentment against an ex-boyfriend because he lied to me. How did I contribute to the situation?

Some possibilities: you picked up on other inconsistencies but let them slide; you knew something sounded "off" but you chose to believe him; you trusted him before you knew him well enough to justify that trust.

The purpose behind looking at your part in a resentment is that it helps you see a pattern in your own behavior that may be inviting these situations into your life.

Since you cannot do anything about your ex-boyfriend's choice to lie, you can only look at your own participation and change your own behavior.

Second, accept that you may never understand "why."

As women, we want to understand WHY someone hurt us – how could he do that? How could she say that? After all I've done!

Even if the person were to explain himself or herself to you truthfully, you probably wouldn't understand the answer, or it would hurt even more.

Also, people who lie, cheat, and steal are by definition liars, so getting an honest explanation is unlikely.

But, in an alternate universe, let's say you can ask your spouse why he cheated on you and he will give you an honest answer. Do you really think you'll feel better if he says, "She's hot." Or, "I was bored." Or, "I don't know...it just was what I wanted to do." Or, "I just didn't think about your feelings."

We will turn over every little detail of a situation or relationship and replay every word and every move to try to discover what went wrong and what we could have done differently to avoid it.

If you 're going to have people in your life, you're going to get hurt. You need to have boundaries, and be accountable for your own behavior (Fourth Step!), but even when you do everything right, you may still end up being hurt, betrayed, or taken advantage of.

Why does this happen? Because people are flawed.

I've hurt and betrayed people – not intentionally, but I'm sure they felt that way. I don't believe "everything happens for a reason," but I do believe that there is a lesson to be learned in every situation.

Look for your lesson, learn the lesson, and move on (lest you be given another test!).

When I feel my mind spinning around the details of a wound, trying to dissect it and figure out what happened, I have to stop.

Jesus said, "No one who puts his hand to the plow and looks back is fit for the kingdom." (See Luke 9:62)

You cannot move forward if you are trying to figure out what happened "back there."

You can't even have peace TODAY when you're trying to figure out the other person's reasons, motivations, what really happened, etc.

We think if we understand it, we'll feel better or we can change the outcome or avoid future pain, but sometimes we have to accept that people do things that hurt us and we don't know why.

Third, stop talking about it all the time. Again, for women, this is tough.

We bond with and nurture others verbally. When you're hurting, you want to feel better, so you tell everybody what's going on, or at least an abridged version of the drama so they will soothe you.

We may even take to social media to vent our hurt so our hundreds of virtual friends can rally around us.

I have learned the hard way: don't do this. Have a few close friends with whom you are honest and with whom you can be transparent about your experiences and feelings. Then, give everybody else the "spin" version.

In public relations, we "spin" a story to make our client or company look better.

For example, the CEO's version of being fired is that he or she decided to pursue other opportunities. (After being fired.)

I recently went through some hurt feelings, and when I saw one of my friends in the hallway at work, I quietly told her I'd ended a relationship, but I was doing fine.

I wasn't really feeling "fine" at the moment, but that is the script I will stick to in public. Sometimes you have to "act as if."

With my mother, my therapist, or my closest girlfriends, I will share the gory details of my pain. Everybody else gets a version that is "spun" to not sound so dramatic.

Really – do you want everybody to know you got dumped? You were cheated on? Your best client left you for the competition? You think YES – I want them to know how mistreated I am and then they'll feel sorry for me. However, that never helps you in the long run.

Why do you want people looking at you wondering why you got dumped? What did you do wrong that your client went to your competitor? Just say, "we're not seeing each other anymore," or "we're not on a contract right now."

When we keep talking about the hurt, we keep picking open the wound. Yes, you need to work through it and talk it out, but don't keep languaging yourself into more pain.

Sometimes you have to look hard for the treat within the trick. Every trick has some One-Derful lesson you can use to make you stronger and smarter moving forward. Focus on that treat!

Raise Your Standards

Ladies, we have a situation. Single women are out-earning single men. While this is good news in terms of gender equality, it's bad news if you're looking for a husband.

This trend of women out-earning men means that there are fewer professional, higher-income men available, and the women feel like they have to compete aggressively to "snag" them. This is a fantastic situation for the men, because they have women falling all over them.

In fact, more and more men in our society are becoming accustomed to aggressive women.

Girls are maturing even faster than boys (due in part to the xenoestrogens in our environment), which means they are interested in relationships earlier than boys are. Thus, the girls chase the boys at younger and younger ages, which is producing a crop of boys and men who don't have to work very hard to get a girlfriend or a wife.

In case you think lowering your standards is a good solution, I'd like to share with you my own experiences of low standards.

For years, people have speculated that I am single because I "must be too picky." In fact, the opposite was true: I was the "make it work girl."

I wasted years dating men who were not compatible with me in a variety of areas, or for whom I just didn't have feelings.

I'm not suggesting that you set your own personal dating bar so high that you eliminate every prospective gentlemen. But please set it higher than I did!

I think we can all agree these are deal-breakers: criminal record; loss of driver's license due to drug crime or DUI; unemployed; drug user; or, abuse of any kind (physical, mental, emotional).

While I did raise my bar higher a few years ago, I recently went through a 15-month dating period where I learned I needed to raise it again in some key areas. These may not be important to you, but if they are, feel free to borrow them.

Spirituality. I want to be with someone with whom I am "equally yoked." Yes, a Christian, but someone who actually has a relationship with God. Less legalistic and more in touch with Spirit.

I want someone who will go to church with me, and who is actually trying to live a life that follows Christ. My spiritual life is very important to me, and I want someone I can share that with.

We don't have to agree on every little thing (or even every big thing), but we have to share core beliefs. I want to live a Spirit-led life. How can I trust a man to lead if he doesn't even know God?

Finances. This one is tricky. If you say you want someone who is financially secure, you risk being called a "gold digger." I don't need someone to pay my bills, but I do want someone who is paying his own bills and can join me in my lifestyle (maybe even raise it a bit).

When you're in your 20's, there may be something romantic about starting out with nothing and building a life together. However, now that I'm in my 40's, I'm not willing to go backwards to bring someone else forward.

No retirement savings? Trashed credit score? Lots of debt? Income that doesn't allow you to support yourself? I'll pass.

The number one area couples fight over is money – I don't want to start off a relationship with that kind of stress, facing a future of financial insecurity.

Career. I've had married girlfriends tell me they wouldn't mind what a man's job was, but it turns out that they're all married to professors, managers, and executives!

I have a successful career – not a job. I want a man who has a career, not just a job. Here's the difference: installing heat pumps is a job; owning the company is a career. Driving a truck is a job; owning a fleet of trucks is a career. Retail sales is a job; selling advertising, financial services, real estate, or insurance is a career.

A "job" implies hourly wages (not the hourly wages of a nurse, doctor, or lawyer, mind you), and a lack of seniority or longevity. Yes, a "job" is better than unemployed, but I'm a career girl – I need a man with a career.

There's no shame in a working man's hustle - I'm not throwing shade at anyone who works! But I want to be with someone that I'm compatible with professionally.

Chemistry. I think this is one area where women are tempted to settle. If your idea of a good relationship is someone who has all of the above traits (or whatever is important to you), and is a great friend, but you're not especially crazy about, then go for it.

Personally, I need to feel attracted to my boyfriend, not merely fond of him. I know chemistry may level out after a while, but why start off with zero passion?

So, I am clear on my own personal standards for dating. I admit – my pool of prospective dates is much smaller, but I'm no longer wasting time on dates with men who have been divorced four times (yes – four. Really.), declared bankruptcy, or are living with their mothers.

My life is pretty One-Derful right now. While I definitely would like someone to share it with, I'd rather keep flying solo than settle for "not quite what I want."

As Dr. Phil says, "I have a standard; either you meet it, or you don't." Doesn't mean you're not a nice guy, it just means you're not the right guy for me.

What is Your Emotional Age?

Recently, I was visiting with a friend of mine and we were sharing that we wouldn't want to revisit our 20's for anything! I agreed with her when she said, "Life is so much better in your 40's!"

I'm all for looking younger (exception: if you're over 45, you probably should not be wearing miniskirts or anything neon), but I'm concerned about the advice we hear today about NOT acting your age.

We seem to be in a culture of perpetual adolescence (do what makes you happy!), but we seem to be more discontented than ever before.

I've been going through an emotional growth spurt, and I've learned that joyful grown-ups are emotionally mature.

Emotional maturity is the foundation for true stability regardless of your circumstances. When you're emotionally mature, you are able to be joyful in spite of situations.

Read on to see if you fit into any of these emotionally immature stages:

THE TODDLER: Emotional toddlers have to rely on others for all of their emotional needs. They are exhausting and high-maintenance. They never ask you how you're doing, mostly because they are solely focused on themselves.

However, if you are struggling, they will be concerned because they recognize you will not be able to focus on them if you are not operating at 100%.

Emotional toddlers throw regular temper tantrums when they are not getting their way in life.

Emotional toddlers don't realize there's anything wrong with their behavior, partly because it gets them their desired results: people do what they want them to do.

They are manipulative and the people around them work hard to keep them from getting upset. After all, doesn't everybody want to short-circuit a toddler's temper tantrum?

THE TEENAGER: Emotional adolescents are moody. They are focused on feeling "happy," but they are not willing to do the work to achieve their emotional goals.

They are emotionally lazy. They want closer relationships, but they're not willing to take time to get to know people.

They want peace, but they are not willing to resolve conflict in a mature way.

They are emotional takers, not givers.

Emotional adolescents don't take responsibility for their behavior and the thoughts and feelings that create the behavior.

They may be aware there is a problem, but they don't know what it is.

THE YOUNG ADULT: Emotional young adults are slightly more advanced than the other two groups, but they are grounded in fear.

They are afraid of failure, afraid of rejection, and afraid of emotional mistakes.

If they are aware of issues in their lives, they generally blame others rather than taking responsibility for where they are in life.

Conversely, emotional ADULTS take responsibility for where they are in life.

For many years, I blamed by parents for not setting me up for success in my relationships.

However, I lived under my parents' "roof" for 20 years; I have been on my own for 23 years. In other words, I've been responsible for my life longer than they were.

Incidentally, my parents did a great job and had a healthy marriage. Guess who dropped the ball? (Spoiler alert: it was me!)

Emotional adults are not afraid to feel negative feelings. They are able and willing to identify and admit their feelings, and then they are able to communicate them honestly to themselves and others (when appropriate).

That's another hallmark of emotional maturity: adults don't dump their moods and feelings on everyone around them.

There's nothing wrong with sharing a problem with a friend, but when you've been sharing the same problem for 6 months and it's not getting better, it's time to stop talking about it. Plus, you're probably wearing your friend out with your broken record of complaining.

My therapist reminded me once that there's only one common denominator in all of my failed relationships: it's me (not the "jerks" I kept giving my phone number to). There's only one common denominator in your unhappiness: YOU.

There's only one common denominator in your undesirable results: YOU.

If you want a One-Derful Life, it's not going to happen when everything goes your way.

That One-Derful Life of peace and purpose happens when you are emotionally mature and can take responsibility for your life. You're no longer an emotional child or a victim, and that's something worth celebrating!

When Nothing Goes Right

We've all had days where it felt like things weren't going our way. Sometimes, we take those days and string them together to form a week, or even months.

It can be deeply frustrating when you're doing the right thing, but you're not getting results.

In weight loss, the dreaded "plateau" occurs when your healthy eating and diligent exercise bring you to a point where your body no longer responds and you stop losing weight. You're doing the right things, but you're not seeing results.

Sometimes a plateau is just a slowdown. You can eat right and exercise, see no movement on the scale for three weeks, then suddenly you lose two pounds. There are changes occurring, but they're so small that you cannot perceive them.

You go on 15 sales calls and nobody wants to buy, then two weeks later, eight new orders come in.

During a plateau, we normally have the opportunity to practice patience, and patience is an excruciating trait to develop because we live in a world that values and delivers instantaneous results.

If you've had a season (whether one day or several years) where it seems like you've hit a plateau – whether in relationships, finances, career, health, or anything else – here are some ideas to help you cope until things start moving again.

This is what is supposed to be happening. Thought leader Marie Forleo suggests that we respond to life's curve balls by saying, "And this is exactly what I wanted."

Personally, I cannot say that with any authenticity, but I do say, "And this is exactly what was supposed to happen."

If it happened, it happened, so railing against the reality of "it" happening won't make "it" un-happen. Which leads me to...

Don't try to figure out "why." I HATE IT when people say, "Everything happens for a reason." No it doesn't.

Can we learn from any experience? Yes. But bad things happen because that is life. We want to believe "everything happens for a reason" because then we can parse some sense of control out of things we don't like.

Please don't ever tell someone who has lost a child that "it happened for a reason."

Now, if you've gained 50 pounds in 4 weeks, you may want to ask, "Why?" But many times in life the answer is going to be, "Because."

Learn to discern the difference between what you can control and what you can't. If you can do something, do it. Otherwise, you're going to need to get comfortable with the idea of acceptance.

Be persistent and consistent in doing the right thing. Not asking why doesn't mean you have to just sit around. Keep doing the right thing, and be consistent and persistent.

You're not going to see a fitness model physique after 3 workouts. You're not going to lose 20 pounds if you eat right for two days.

If you're not seeing results, but you know you are doing the right thing, you have to keep at it.

It's like that weight loss example: all of a sudden, you see the results, but if you start wallowing in cheesecake those results will never come (trust me).

Abandon the fast food mentality.

We have been conditioned to expect fast results. Microwaves, text messages, electronic payments, Amazon Prime, and dry shampoo have trained us to believe we can get what we want, when we want it.

Unfortunately, the Universe does not work like that.

You may have heard one of my favorite sayings: God is never late, but He's usually not early, either.

Haven't you noticed that God's timetable is rarely as fast as ours?

Every day for my snack, I eat an apple. I wondered if I could grow my own apples, and it turns out that if I planted an apple tree from seed, it would be two to five years before I'd see any fruit. Five years! And between now and then I would have to consistently and persistently care for that tree.

Sometimes, when YOU aren't seeing results, it's because God is behind the scenes, working out everything for YOUR highest good.

Find joy in the process. You had better figure out how to enjoy the trip.

One time, I was flying to Paris and a delayed flight stranded me in Atlanta. I knew I had a choice: be upset or enjoy myself. I chose to enjoy myself because there are enough times where I don't recognize that I have a choice; so, if I can choose happiness, I will.

When I go to see my doctor, I know I'm going to wait. I bring a book to read or work to do and use that waiting time as time to lose myself in a story or to catch up on grading. That way, I appreciate – rather than resent – the waiting time.

You're going to have times where you have to wait on things in your life. Are you going to choose to wait in misery or will you choose to make that wait more pleasant for yourself? Because you do have a choice.

Choosing to see things differently can help you move from feeling that nothing is going right to starting to see your own One-Derful Life develop.

Eliminate Second Hand Stress

I recently heard a term I've never heard before: second-hand stress. There was no further explanation, so I was left to ponder it alone.

The phrase that came to mind was "second-hand smoke."

Second-hand smoke is a toxic by-product of another person's unhealthy behavior: smoking. Have you ever seen a car driving by with the windows rolled up, an occupant smoking, and a child as a passenger? It seems somehow negligent to "trap" a child with second-hand smoke.

Using that logic, second-hand stress must be the toxic by-product of another person's unhealthy behavior.

Have you ever felt trapped in someone else's drama? You have no influence or control over the situation, but you feel all of the stress and negativity from whatever is happening. It's like being trapped in a moving car full of smoke – you can't breathe, you can't see clearly, and you can't get out.

As adults, we have the ability to say to a friend or family member who smokes, "you cannot smoke in my car," or "you cannot smoke in the house," or "if you're going to smoke, I'm leaving."

That's why it's disturbing to see a child in that smoky car: the child cannot set those boundaries.

I find it interesting that I frequently feel as though I have no control or influence over the second-hand stress in my life. I'm usually afraid I'll upset the "smoker" by setting a boundary to protect my mental and emotional health.

Yet, many of us tend to be pretty feisty when we're setting boundaries with cigarette smokers! I certainly don't have a problem telling people not to smoke around me!

Unlike a child, you do have control over what you allow into your life in terms of other people's drama.

Sometimes you have to tell people you cannot tolerate their emotional "smoke."

A friend of mine had to set this boundary with me one year. I was struggling with a lot of painful situations, and my friend got to the point where she felt very helpless and overwhelmed with the level of drama I was dealing with. It was good that she set that boundary with me, as it caused me to seek more solutions to resolve my circumstances. Her ability to set that boundary to protect her own mental health from my second-hand stress set an example for me in setting boundaries in my own life.

If you're a non-smoker, you probably wouldn't let someone into your house, bring out the ashtrays, and encourage her to light up.

I just about hit the roof when some workmen were smoking at the opening of my crawlspace; the fumes were coming right up through the torn-up floor!

When it comes to second-hand stress, that's exactly what we do: throw open the doors of our hearts, and invite people in who are going to trash the place and pollute the air with their drama and negativity.

How do you know if it's second-hand stress or not? My feeling is that YOUR stress is stress that results from YOUR behavior.

For example, if you take on too much, you may feel stressed and overwhelmed. That is a consequence of your own choices.

However, if you're afraid to answer the phone every time a certain person calls because you're afraid to hear about "what the problem is now," that may be second-hand stress.

Just like a smoker isn't going to stop smoking just because YOU don't like it, the people in your life aren't going to stop dumping their drama on you – especially if you have trained them that you are available to be their emotional garbage dump.

Obviously, if you have a minor child, that child's behavior may cause stress for you – that's part of the job description of "parent."

However, when you are dealing with an adult, you don't need to suffer through the consequences of someone else's choices. Unless you enjoy second-hand stress, of course.

I've been looking at some areas in my life where I may have second-hand stress, and I'm seeing where I need to set some boundaries. In the same way I prefer to nicely ask a smoker not to light up rather than dump my drink on his head, I prefer to have a loving conversation with my emotional "smoker" than just explode in anger.

You're not a helpless child in a smoke-filled car. You are an adult, and you have the right to set boundaries to protect your heart and mind from the toxic second-hand stress of another person's unhealthy behavior. Get out of the car!

The Reason You May Be Single

Warning: this may hurt your feelings. Proceed at your own risk.

I don't have children, but my best friend has a 5-year old and a 2-year old, so I am learning a lot about temper tantrums.

Recently, her 5-year old daughter through one humdinger of a hissy fit while at school. Here's how our conversation went:

Me: Yikes. Sounds embarrassing. Did you give in just to get her to be quiet?

BFF: No way. If you give in, the kid learns two things: (1) the temper tantrum is effective; and, (2) they're in charge.

Valuable information. Parents learn not to give in to temper tantrums because it's not good for the child to learn to handle the "bad" things in life (i.e., not getting your way) by acting out.

So here's the question: do you think your Heavenly Father will give in to your spiritual temper tantrum?

Well, you say, I'm a mature, spiritual woman – I don't throw hissy fits anymore. I'll bet you do (we all do). See if any of these sound familiar:

Why doesn't he like me (love me, want me)?? I've given him everything. We could be so happy together if only.....

How come the girls who run around with married men end up getting married and I'm still alone?

I'll never be happy if I don't find someone.

I wish I had a boyfriend....

Other forms of the temper tantrum: snarky comments about your friends who get engaged; trashing your ex all over town; holding onto anger and bitterness about failed or non-existent relationships.

Let's be clear: God will not reward that behavior by giving you what you want.

On the spiritual plane, the universe is not invested in your stagnation or in furthering anger and despair.

God wants you to live, flourish, prosper, and be abundant.

"But I'm not prosperous in dating – no one ever asks me out." Well, here's a fact: most guys don't like angry women.

I love the book of Jonah. We all know about the giant fish and Nineveh, but I find a lesson in Jonah's temper tantrum.

The Lord sends Jonah to warn the Ninevites that He's angry and is going to destroy the city. The people listen to Jonah and repent, so God spares the city.

After that victory, Jonah throws a temper tantrum (see Jonah chapter 4). You can read the story for yourself, but I would like to take some creative license and re-write the scene for us single girls.

I will use myself in the role of "Jonah" because I've played this part before.

Mary: This is what always happens, God. I have to watch EVERYBODY else find someone and get married and I'm stuck being a stupid bridesmaid. What's the point? I just wish I was dead, and I might as well be since I'm going to be an old spinster.

God: Why are you angry?

Mary: (Goes into the den with a pint of Ben & Jerry's and plops down on the couch to watch Netflix while bingeing on sugary dairy foods.) If I'm going to be alone, it doesn't matter if I get fat.

The phone rings and it's a friend who wants to go see a movie, but I respond that I'm too depressed and just need to be alone.

Mary: I wish I had someone to watch TV with me.

God: I send you good friends who want your company, but you can't enjoy anything in your life because you're angry over everybody else's "good fortune" in relationships. You don't even tend to the ones you have now, why should I send more?

And, scene.

I know you don't want more girlfriends or platonic guy friends, but maybe the Lord is sending you these people because you're not ready for something else.

We always want to think He's getting us ready for some super-fantastic guy, but maybe God's protecting that guy FROM YOU.

Are you missing out on the good things in your life right now because you're throwing temper tantrum with God because you're not getting your way?

I'm not sure I believe God grants us EVERY desire in our heart. Jeremiah says the "heart is deceitful above all things." King David (as detailed in 1 Chronicles 28:2) had it as his heart's desire to build the Lord's temple – sounds pretty good and noble, but God said no. David had to content himself with storing up the supplies, because Solomon was to build the temple. Just because you want something really badly, it may not mean God is going to give it to you.

Meanwhile, you should be enjoying your life. Believe me, no one wants to follow a spiritual path when they see us as angry, bitter, and disconnected from life.

And men won't want to be around you if they pick up on that temper tantrum (and they will – men are very perceptive in their own way).

No more temper tantrums. Part of spiritual maturity is disciplining yourself not to pull that stuff with God. He won't reward your bad attitude.

Put down the ice cream and plug into the life you have now. If you do, you'll find it's probably already pretty One-Derful.

Taking Responsibility

Recently I asked a couple of my students who are in trouble academically what caused them to fail their classes last semester. Their answer: "bad teachers."

As adults, we probably can all react to that statement with a resounding, "Yeah, right."

But, we have our own versions of that belief; such as, "I can't be successful at work because my boss (or coworker) is a jerk." "I can't be happy at home because of my spouse (or lack of one)." "I can't have the life I want because of my kids (or lack of kids)."

One of the most difficult things to do is to see how we have participated in the creation of our circumstances and to take responsibility for how things have unfolded in our lives.

How many times have you wished for a "different life," or that things would change in some area (home, relationships, finances, career)?

If you want to see change in your life, you have to focus on what you can control. You can't control other people or their behavior, but you can always control your own responses and your own actions.

You are responsible for your thoughts, words, and actions. Most of us don't realize there's a constant internal dialogue running inside our heads.

It's estimated that we think 80,000 to 90,000 thoughts per day and that the majority of those are repeated thoughts from yesterday. And the majority of those repeated thoughts are negative.

Sadly, our thoughts come out as words (either spoken, texted, or posted on social media) or manifest as actions.

If you spend the entire day thinking about how upset you are over something, you are very likely to snap at your kids or soothe yourself with alcohol or cookies.

St. Paul said we must "take every thought captive and make it obedient to Christ." (See 2 Corinthians 10:5.)

How do you do this? Author Byron Katie suggests that we ask questions; for example, "Is this true?"

When you think, "My boss is a jerk," ask, "Is that true? Is he really a jerk?" Your internal dialogue may say that it is, but if you look at things through your boss's eyes, you may see that he or she is trying to do their best.

Maybe they were a jerk to you because you were disrespectful. Let's say your boss really is a jerk. Does thinking about this over and over empower you or does it make you a victim? (Spoiler alert: it makes you a victim.)

If you're struggling with singleness, is it really true that you're going to be alone forever? You can only answer yes if you are able to see the future; in which case, please drop everything and play the lottery.

But it may become true if you meditate on the woes of "being alone forever" because you will act in a way that will make that true and those actions will repel the very love you long for.

Today is evidence of yesterday's thoughts and behaviors, and tomorrow is going to be evidence of today's thoughts and behaviors.

If you eat a cheesecake every day for 30 days, you are going to gain weight. It may seem like it happened "all of a sudden," but when you look back, you'll see that your weight gain was due to a sustained, unhealthy pattern of behavior.

If you feel bitter about anything, I can promise you it is because you have mentally engaged in negative thoughts up until today about that subject.

Here's a technique I learned to erase bitterness that works. Author Marianne Williamson says to pray for the happiness and peace of the person you are angry at for 5 minutes a day for 30 days. At the end of that time, either they will have changed, or you won't care anymore.

I have found that to be true. Most of the time, the other person doesn't change, but my attitude changes and that may spark a different reaction from the person.

Here's how to figure out what you need to take responsibility for: borrow this exercise from the Fourth Step of Alcoholics Anonymous.

In AA, recovering alcoholics are instructed to make a list of the people they resent and the reason they resent the person. Many report this is the fun part. The list is written, not mental.

Next, go through each person and circumstance and write down what YOU contributed to the situation.

For example, if your resentment is against your ex-boyfriend because he cheated on you, you might find that your contribution was that you ignored red flags early on, or you had an unrealistic expectation of his behavior, or you trusted someone you shouldn't have trusted.

If you resent your boss because you were passed over for a promotion you believe you deserved, your contribution may be that you expected the promotion system to be merit-based and didn't think organizational politics would affect you.

No matter what the situation is, you have contributed something to it. Did you contribute to your abuse as a child? NO - of course not. But you may be continuing to victimize yourself now if you have not dealt with the past.

Ask, what can you do to change what you are able to change? The good news is, you can probably change a lot of things.

Let's say you are miserable at work because you resent your boss because he promoted someone else instead of you.

Begin with praying for your boss and your newly-promoted coworker for 5 minutes a day for 30 days. Pray that they will be happy, peaceful, and blessed. You won't "feel" like doing this - it's an action step, not an emotion.

Pray for the willingness to see the situation differently. A Course in Miracles says, "the Holy Spirit responds fully to our slightest invitation."

You choose your actions: you can be salty and bitter and unpleasant at work - which will guarantee you don't get a promotion later and will also confirm to your boss that he made the right decision in NOT promoting you.

Or, you can choose to be pleasant and do your best. If that is not possible for you, you can look for a new job. Remember: you are completely at choice in how you act. And, today's actions will determine the results you get tomorrow.

We get a lot of support in society today to believe things are not our responsibility. Your parents messed you up, other people don't respect you, elected leaders are making bad decisions.

But each of us has the ability to decide how we are going to play the cards we are being dealt.

Taking responsibility is the first step in having a truly One-Derful Life.

When Will This Be Over?

One year, I reflected that I had spent the majority of the year worried, anxious, and grieving.

Even more sadly, I saw that my fretting, worrying, and resisting the events of life had only served to undermine my own sense of stability. For all my pleading and crying and trying to "get a handle on things," people and events did not respond to my liking.

The ladies in my Bible study group told me that "good will come from it," but every time they said that, I bucked against the sentiment.

One night, I defiantly told them "there's nothing good about losing a loved one to suicide."

Everybody experiences grief in one way or another, and my friend Linda was so kind and gentle in her response. "You're right, Mary – that loss isn't a good thing, but God can use that tragedy to bring out good things in YOU."

She should know: she lost her only son in a car accident when he was only 16.

Recently, I was studying 1 Corinthians 10:13: "No temptation has seized you except what is common to man. And God is faithful; he will not let you be tempted beyond what you can bear. But when you are tempted, he will also provide a way out so that you can stand up under it."(NIV)

The Greek word for temptation is *peirasmos,* which means "trial with a beneficial purpose and effect." (Strong's Greek Dictionary)

So, let's substitute: "No trial with a beneficial purpose and effect has seized you except what is common to man. And God is faithful; he will not let you be tried with a beneficial purpose and effect beyond what you can bear. But when you are tried with a beneficial purpose and effect, he will also provide a way out so that you can stand up under it."

No trial has seized you except what is common to man. Everybody struggles and suffers.

Nobody gets the perfect life they imagined. They may get the perfect life YOU imagined for yourself, but nobody has a life without trial – it is common to man.

Are you the only person who is lonely? Are you the only person who is grieving? Are you the only person who feels abandoned? Are you the only person who thinks, "If only things were different, I would be ok." No.

As long as I resist my trials (or sufferings or losses or *peirasmoses* – many apologies to the Greek language), I keep myself in a state of turmoil.

Even if this one goes away, soon another will take its place. Once you get the house organized, things fall apart at work. Things get better at work, and your relationship ends. You get a new boyfriend, and then there's a health scare. You get healed, and the house needs a new roof.

"He will ALSO provide a way out so that you can STAND UP under it (emphasis added)."

There's a lot of help in those 15 words. God will provide the way out – you don't have to struggle and strain and try to solve it yourself. He will Himself provide that solution at the time of the trial.

That doesn't mean you will have instant knowledge of the outcome, but it means that the solution is there – be patient and dig in with God until the solution presents itself.

God wants us to be able to STAND UP even under the weight of the trial. He doesn't want us bowed over, crawling, and defeated.

At some point, you have to decide if you are going to keep longing for the life you want, or if you are going to start living the life you currently have.

There are things we can control and things we can change.

One year, I cleaned out every drawer, every closet, and the attic. I lost 20 pounds and renovated the floors in my house. I let go of toxic relationships and strengthened relationships with people who had really been there for me. Those are the areas of life that I can change.

I can't change who dies and who lives. I can't change HOW others live. I can't change many of the circumstances of my past and present.

But, I can be open to the good that God can work in me, if only I remain willing to experience it.

Author Mark Nepo writes, "When we are broken, perhaps we are being broken open."

That resonates in my spirit. God isn't trying to break us, maybe He wants to break us open so that good things can get in and good things can come out.

The greatest gift we can receive is not a ring, or a car, or the latest gadget.

If you feel heartbroken during this season of your life, consider the possibility that you are being broken open by a faithful God who is right now providing the way for you to stand up under this trial that will end in a beneficial purpose and a good effect FOR YOU.

The Single Gal's Guide to Wisdom

I heard a definition of wisdom once that I love: wisdom is the ability to manage life and to make good decisions.

In today's culture, it's easy to fall into the trap of believing that you can't have a full and complete life if you're single.

Most of our popular movies, television programs, literature, and advertising images are centered around the idea that you need to find that one special someone who will save you from your life, complete you (thanks, "Jerry Maguire"), and set you on the path towards happily ever after.

And, by the way, we will sell you lots of products to help you find them faster.

If you're single now, it's a possibility that you will remain single. However, between the high divorce rate (nearly 50% on first marriages) and the biological fact that women outlive men by an average of 7 years, it is highly probable that many married women will become single again.

Either way, you want to have a happy life – everybody wants to feel secure, have peace, and be happy.

If you are hoping to "find someone", I can promise you that men are very attracted to women who have their lives in order and who can live independently and confidently. Plus, if you already have a great life, you won't desperately settle for a man who ends up not being such a great guy.

So, here are some words of wisdom to help my single girls as you make your way in the world.

TIP #1 - Friends are NOT Forever.

I used to say, "Men come and go, but your friends are forever."

Most of us have experienced the "breakup" of a friendship with a gal pal, and I think it's worse than the end of any romantic relationship.

People grow and change. We mature in our opinions and attitudes, we have new life experiences, our priorities change.

If you have one friend that you remain in relationship with for your entire life, you are in the minority.

Some of the friendships that were really important to me a few years ago, are not so healthy for me now.

I used to believe that friendships had to last for a lifetime, but now I view them as I would an article of clothing – I probably don't need to hang on to it forever.

One of you may outgrow the relationship. Maybe it will be you, maybe it will be your friend.

Relationships go through seasons – sometimes you're close as can be, other times you drift away.

One way to have healthy friendships is to diversify – have several friendships.

My "best friend" has been my BFF for about 8 years now. When she started having children, I was very afraid that she would leave me behind and want friends who were moms. She was afraid I wouldn't want to be her friend because she'd be a "boring mom" (her words, not mine).

Over the years, our relationship has changed. No, we don't go out for "girls night" very often. We opt for lunch, instead.

Sometimes I get tired of hearing stories about her kids, and sometimes she wishes I would offer to babysit.

We have had to adapt to our new life circumstances, but she still holds the "best friend" title. We have grown into a different kind of friendship.

Because my bestie isn't as available now that she has kids, I have added in some additional friends. But no one person is going to be a perfect fit for every area of your life.

Stop looking for the "perfect friend" who you can do everything with and expand your collection.

I go to the movies with Katie (but her favorite genre is horror, which horrifies me, so she always has to ask another friend to go to those); I attend the symphony with Becky; I watch sports with Terri; I talk about spirituality with Nancy; I eat sushi with Julia; I shop with Shawna. See – find a different friend for the different aspects of your life.

Diversifying in this way will also protect you when you have problems in a friendship. This way, when one of my friends is busy with work or a new boyfriend, I don't feel lonely – I just call another gal.

And if a friendship is fading, let it go – maybe it will come back, or maybe it's time for it to fade away. Don't be afraid to let go – you will find new friends.

The best way to find friends? I was told, "If you want a friend, be a friend." There are a lot of lonely people in the world – reach out and be a friend.

TIP #2 – Get Your Financial House in Order. I could fill up a very long book with advice on managing your finances, but let me sum up the basics with this: live beneath your means. This means you spend less than you make. Period.

Once you are doing that, you have the cash to pay off your debts (critically important) and to save.

You must invest in your retirement and plan for your future. Don't know how to do that?

Start reading. Pick up a book on the subject at the library or bookstore – I recommend any of the *Rich Dad, Poor Dad* books by Robert Kiyosaki or *The Millionaire Next Door* by Thomas J. Stanley and William D. Danko.

Go see a Certified Financial Planner or Certified Financial Analyst for some face-to-face guidance.

Don't wait around hoping a man will save you financially – you may remain single, or your Prince Charming may not have the financial resources you wanted – be financially healthy regardless of your marital status.

TIP #3 - Take Care of Yourself. It's easy to start thinking there's something wrong with you when you feel like a single in a world of couples.

Almost every single man and woman I know has felt (in the past, or currently) that there is something wrong with him or her.

Now, if there IS something "wrong" with you – work on fixing it. Do the best you can with what you have.

If you're a single woman looking for a man, you need to know that appearance matters because men are visually stimulated.

You don't have to be a supermodel, but spruce up a little bit.

Is your hairstyle flattering? Is your makeup attractive and age-appropriate? Do you look and feel confident in your clothes? Do you look friendly and approachable?

You also need to take care of yourself beyond the physical.

Finding a mate isn't going to change who you are. If you're not happy now, you won't be happy with the guy of your dreams. As I've said many times before, your dream guy probably won't be attracted to you in your depressed state. Men like happy women.

Do whatever you need to do to have a happy, joyful life right now – that is the best way to attract love. And, even if you don't meet Mr. Right, YOU'LL feel better!

Eat right, exercise, put your home in order, clean out your car, find a therapist, volunteer, adopt a pet, take up meditation, get involved in

SOMETHING healthy and positive – this will help you be happy whether or not you end up as part of a couple.

Stop playing the "there's something wrong with me" tape in your head. Change what you think needs changing, and then just accept yourself for who you are.

If you need a romantic relationship to validate that you are ok, you will never experience peace and security because that person will constantly have to reassure you, and most people get weary of that kind of insecurity. They leave, and you are devastated.

Don't put your happiness, peace, and joy on hold until Prince Charming shows up. Live NOW, and even if he is delayed for a while, you won't notice because you'll be loving life. Your One-Derful Life.

Trick or Truth?

Over the years, I have heard, and fallen for, a variety of untrue statements. Sometimes, I've had people use my singleness as a way to get me to work for their organization – "come volunteer with us – maybe you'll meet your future husband!"

Some of these falsehoods are based in popular culture, some come out of church communities, and some are just wishful thinking.

So here we go – time to shed some light on the tricks single girls fall for.

Trick: God plants desires in your heart, so if you really want something, you'll get it.

Truth: There are godly desires. There are also desires that are pleasing to God, but God doesn't necessarily fulfill them.

Sometimes those desires are left unfulfilled because we stand in the way, and sometimes they are left unfulfilled because they aren't in God's plan for our lives.

King David had the desire to build the Lord's temple, but God would not allow him to; instead, the Lord ordained for David's son, Solomon, to build the temple. David's desire was Godly, but it wasn't in God's plan.

God created us for fellowship and companionship, but not everybody is meant to be married (Jesus said that!).

This line of thinking would suggest that just because I REALLY want to binge out and eat an entire chocolate cake in one sitting, that desire must be from God.

And, while I do believe that chocolate was created by God Himself, I'm pretty sure that abusing the temple of the Holy Spirit by eating an entire cake is not part of God's plan for me or my thighs.

That's like saying God wants you to abuse alcohol or drugs just because you have an addiction that you didn't ask for.

However, I do believe that if you're seeking after His will for your life, you will begin to focus more on following God's plan, even if that means you have to let your own plan go.

Ultimately, it's been my experience that He will change your heart and make you alright with the situation. Maybe it wouldn't be your Plan A, but if you trust God's plan is better than yours, you will have peace.

Trick: My soul mate accidentally married the wrong person.

Truth: A lot of people (around 50% of first marriages, in fact) feel that their marriage was a mistake.

However, if the man you're "in love with" is currently married or in a committed relationship with someone else, he's not YOUR soul mate.

I know you feel a lot of chemistry and you think it's meant to be – if only he hadn't accidentally married the wrong girl!

If his marriage is a "mistake", let him get out of it WITHOUT YOUR INVOLVEMENT.

You should know that 95% of all marriages that begin as extramarital affairs end in divorce.

And let's call it what it is: adultery. It's wrong, no matter what your religious or spiritual beliefs are.

It's not okay to take things that don't belong to you. It doesn't matter that his wife cheated on him, they don't sleep together anymore, they're staying together for the kids (all his version of events, by the way) – he's choosing to stay married to her.

By the way – haven't you noticed how married men will say they can't get a divorce because it would destroy their children, but they're okay with cheating on their children's mother and destroying her that way? Like, a divorce would destroy her but infidelity is okay. Don't fall for it.

Do you really believe God is sending you a married man when every spiritual discipline, path, and belief system says it's wrong? Or, maybe you're the one exception in the universe to the "do not commit adultery" commandment.

Tell him to call you when he's legally single. You're better off sitting at home alone than destroying another woman's relationship.

Call it karma, but you will reap what you sow. If you destroy a family, don't think God is obligated to bless you.

Trick: Younger men like older women.

Truth: Ah, yes. The "cougar" theory. Popular entertainment promotes this idea, but it is highly unusual for men to be in long-term partnerships with older women (I'm talking women 5 or more years older).

Here's why: biology. A man's DNA wants to reproduce – that's how we make sure we have an ongoing supply of human beings.

Therefore, his brain tells him younger women are better mates for child bearing. Translation: old chick equals old eggs.

Many times, he'll say an older woman is attractive, sexy, and fun, but he just doesn't want to settle down with her. He may not even know why.

I'll tell you why: his DNA wants viable eggs.

When I share this with my over-40 friends, they are quick to point out the only relationship on the planet that seemed to be working as an example: Ashton Kutcher and Demi Moore.

However, if you look like Demi Moore, you can probably have any man in the world regardless of age.

And, look at how that ended up: they divorced and Ashton Kutcher married the much younger Mila Kunis, with whom he has kids!

Younger men are fun to date, but it is unlikely that you will marry and settle down with one. Also, you look pathetic chasing young guys around – it makes you look desperate.

Trick: He'll wake up in 5 or 10 years and realize I'm the girl for him.

Truth: No, he won't.

One of my most important relationships ended when my beloved left me for his ex-wife (turns out he'd been seeing her behind my back for at least a month). I grieved so intensely, and it was very gratifying when I heard they had broken up.

I was gloating to a male friend of mine when he made a cutting observation: "Yeah, but he still hasn't called YOU."

Men know pretty quickly where they want things to go with you. If you are waiting around for a year or more and he hasn't made any commitment towards moving forward, you are wasting your time.

Sure, he may still want to date you. Maybe hanging out with you is better than being alone. Maybe he wants to keep you around until somebody better comes along.

If you have to sell him on the idea of being with you, you're barking up the wrong tree. Men know what they want and they go after it.

They're never "confused" about which team to pull for, what they want to watch on TV, or how they feel about steroid use in professional sports.

They know which cut of steak they like, they know how to fix things, and they basically still run the world.

He's not going to magically realize how great you are in 10 years. Stop hanging around waiting for him to see the light and get out there and meet someone who will value you.

"What if I never meet anyone?" Well, you definitely won't meet anyone as long as you're hanging out with Mr. Indecisive.

Don't fall for these tricks. The universe is invested in your growth, and God wants you to be happy.

You were given a sound mind for a reason – use it to avoid these tricks, and you'll free yourself up for some real treats. One-Derful treats!

Get Your Boundaries!

As a single woman, I have fallen into the trap of trying to please others to my own detriment.

From my parents and relatives, to friends, to colleagues and superiors (not to mention men I've dated!), I have many times let others' priorities surpass my own.

While St. Paul said, "Consider others better than yourself," (see Philippians 2:3) we have to use wisdom and stay the course in our own lives.

If you're single, you need healthy boundaries to attract and maintain a healthy, loving relationship.

If you're coupled, you need healthy boundaries to be happy and well-rounded as an individual.

One of my favorite authors, Dr. Henry Cloud, has written many books on healthy relationships.

The first book by him that I read was *Boundaries*, and I highly recommend it! It will give you a thorough understanding of what boundaries are and are not, as well as how to set and honor them.

I still struggle in this area because I don't want other people to be mad at me.

I once commented to a mentor that I was a "people pleaser," and she immediately corrected me by showing me that my priority wasn't the other person's happiness or emotional well-being; rather, my priority was to avoid my own negative feelings that would result if I disappointed the other person.

That isn't "people pleasing," it's avoidance and a form of selfishness because I'm not willing to feel badly when someone else doesn't like what I do.

I see this with parents: unwilling to feel the discomfort of setting boundaries with their children because the child will be upset. Rather than feel guilty (or uncomfortable in any form), they let the child have his way. This is the equivalent of kicking the can down the road and it ends up hurting both the child and the parent.

The child doesn't learn or develop life skills and discipline, and the parent develops resentment.

If you've decided to clean up your diet and your best friend pressures you to have a slice of her birthday cake, it's up to you to establish and respect your own boundary. If you don't respect your boundaries, why would anyone else?

If someone doesn't respect your boundaries, that is a red flag: the person may not respect you and may be more interested in controlling and manipulating you. (P.S. – this is a great time to audit your own behavior and be sure you are respecting other people's boundaries as well!)

In dating, it can be tempting to acquiesce to the other person's wishes and desires because we think we can avoid rejection if we go along.

Most women would be surprised to know that the majority of high-quality men respect and enjoy women who have their own opinions and can make good decisions with respect to their own lives. Certainly, you should be kind and loving when setting boundaries, but you don't have to participate in activities that devalue you or derail you from your own goals.

I dated someone for a while who lacked boundaries with an ex-girlfriend. Sadly, I also lacked boundaries and would tolerate him canceling plans with me because she needed something.

I wouldn't say anything when she was calling and texting – interrupting our dates.

Today, if I'm dating someone who cancels plans with me to "help" an ex, I free up his schedule permanently because one of my standards is that I don't prioritize men who are prioritizing other women. (Exception: if she is the mother of any of his children and helping her helps the kids, I'm all for it.)

Another boundary: I turn my phone off (or at least silence the ringer) when I need to work on a project, when I am teaching, and when I am sleeping.

Just because the world is "on" 24/7, I don't have to be constantly interrupted and pressured to respond.

Think others will "freak out" if they can't get a response from you in 29 seconds? Start training them to expect a response when you give one.

One of my mentors has an automatic response on her phone so if you text her while she's driving, you get a reply that reads, "I'm driving right now – I'll get back to you when I'm able." I mean, who would insist that you text them back while they're driving?

Having boundaries isn't about being inflexible or uncompromising – it's about not being willing to compromise on what is important with respect to your values and your life's work.

If I don't feel like having sushi, but my best gal pal is craving it, I may go. However, if one of my friends is dying to go see the latest horror movie I'll pass because I do not want to take in that type of negative imagery.

I am not willing to sacrifice my peace of mind and positive focus in order for a friend to have company at a scary movie.

God has a One-Derful plan for each of us, but we are to be active participants!

St. Paul also said that if he focused on pleasing men, he wouldn't be able to please God (see Galatians 1:10).

I often say, "You can do anything, but you can't do everything." That's where boundaries serve you – they allow you to do what you are called to do.

Don't Break Your Own Heart

I'm certainly not an expert in successful relationships, but I know a lot about relationship fails!

One summer, while in Orange County, California, I connected with a friend of mine.

"Linda" is in her mid 30's, a divorced mom of two, and a successful entrepreneur. Like many of us, she wants to find Mr. Right and couple up.

As an aside, I found it humorous that Linda was complaining about the lack of quality men in Orange County. I've heard women all over the country complain about not being able to meet "decent" guys. However, you can't meet the right man if you're wasting your time and emotional energy on the wrong man! Back to Linda...

She met this guy at a work conference. They spent two whole days together, where he swept her off her feet and promised her their married life together would be domestic bliss.

"I just knew it was right – he was the one," she said breathlessly.

Based on his expertly-delivered script, she decided to rent a hotel room and invited him to join her.

They were enjoying a (ahem) romantic interlude when the phone rang. It was his live-in girlfriend demanding to speak to him. She had found my friend's name on his social media and called the hotel where the conference was being held to track down her man. Awkward!

I was reeling from this story when Linda regaled me with her second attempt in a month to find love.

This time, she drove six hours to Northern California to spend the night with a guy she'd met who once again promised her the moon.

Predictably, once she returned to Orange County, Mr. Wonderful disappeared.

A friend of mine in Texas has spent the past year chasing men who are clearly using her for "booty calls."

She says she takes it for what it is and is okay with it, but the more time she spends with these guys, the more emotionally invested she becomes.

I think gentlemen will back me up when I remind the ladies that once you're in the "One Night Stand" category, you can't crossover to "Wife Material."

Now, you might say that it doesn't matter if you're jumping into these whirlwind courtships because you're willing to take the risk to find love.

Yes, any relationship requires you to risk being vulnerable and risk getting your feelings hurt or being disappointed.

But a healthy relationship will not require you to jump into a physical, emotional, and mental connection with someone you've known for 5 days (or less).

When you think, "I know he's The One," remember that is your brain's dopamine and oxytocin talking. If he's The One, what's the harm in getting to know each other?

I've been on both sides of this experience. I've jumped in and I've gone slowly. Personally, I find the slow approach to be much more successful. What do I mean by that?

First of all, don't sleep with him for at least 90 days (thanks, Steve Harvey!). If he's only interested "in one thing," he won't stick around. Or, he'll be getting it somewhere else and you'll see that you don't have his full attention. If he's a quality man who is looking for a relationship, he'll wait and get to know you.

Most companies have a 90-day probation period before they will permanently hire an employee or extend benefits. The reason: most people can't keep up the good impression for 90 days. That 90-day probation period in a relationship can save you heartache, humiliation, time, and money.

I mentioned dopamine and oxytocin. Dopamine is the brain chemical that gives you a high (like cocaine or chocolate or great shoes or falling in love).

Oxytocin – the "cuddle hormone" is what bonds women to babies and men. Even if you think you're playing it cool, your brain is sabotaging you because it's creating a bond with your partner (unless you are totally not into him, in which case you probably aren't intimate).

This chemical transaction in your brain makes it impossible to see red flags, pick up on things that aren't quite right, or determine if what he's saying and doing match up. Trust me – the inability to think clearly combined with the chemistry will have you in so deep that your heartbreak will be nearly unbearable.

Every time I have broken this self-imposed rule of giving things time, I have suffered greatly.

When I have followed it, I have spared myself much pain and the humiliation of having been rejected by someone I thought cared about me.

It's not just the time wasted in the relationship, it's the time it takes you to recover from the hurt.

And every heartbreak takes a toll and can make it more difficult for you to open up the next time.

Can you undo the damage? Yes. But it's a very deliberate and sometimes lengthy process.

If you want a man to see you as the valuable, One-Derful woman that you are, don't jump in so fast!

Take a few months and get to know this man. If he's Mr. Right, he'll still be here. If he can't make it through the 90-day probation period, he doesn't deserve your benefits!

Clear Out the Clutter and Climb Out of the Gutter

Over the past 18 months, I've been systematically clearing out clutter from my home, my office, and my life.

I found I had 427 pencils (but no pencil sharpener), innumerable pens, and 52 shampoo bottles each with ½ inch of product at the bottom.

I see this decluttering process as a parallel to my mental, emotional, and spiritual growth. I cannot carry everything from my past into my future. Nor do I need everything from my past in my present!

Instead, I have made room for new things. In the meantime, I am enjoying the open spaces in closets and drawers.

Here are some things I've learned:

Stop trying to make do with things that aren't quite right.

My toaster oven was pretty banged up – scratches and rust spots marred the finish, and the tray had turned colors after years of broiling and baking.

Furthermore, the toaster oven didn't toast. The oven function worked fine, but the toasting function was completely dead.

I was at my brother's house in Los Angeles, admiring his new, shiny toaster oven and thinking about my sad, dilapidated one at home.

Then I realized I could go buy a new toaster oven for $25. Light bulb! Revelation! I didn't have to make do with a non-toasting toaster oven!

Yet, I felt strangely guilty about getting rid of it. After all, the oven function worked just fine.

That's what I do in relationships: I keep participating in relationships that aren't quite right or where something is broken.

It's a mentality that "this is what I have now, so I'd better work with this." True, you can't run to the store and get a new boyfriend for $25 (or, maybe you can.....I've never tried), but as long as you're holding on to the old relationship there's no room for the new one to get in.

By the way – I got rid of the old toasterless oven and I love my new, shiny one!

Don't keep painful reminders. I was sorting through some old photos and I found some pictures of a woman I used to be friends with.

These photos were also from a difficult time in my life, and she and I are no longer in communication.

I felt guilty, but I tossed them in the trash. I did keep some photos of us during happier times, but why should I take up room in photo albums with photos that bring up hurtful memories?

I want to keep the good memories from that friendship. If she and I reconnect in the future, I'm sure I can get copies of the photos I tossed!

When you release things you don't want or need, you discover things you didn't realize you had.

I discovered that I have multiple copies of several movies, music CDs I had forgotten about, and lots of tasty recipes I've never tried.

Similarly, I had been holding on to an expectation about a friend who doesn't always treat me very nicely.

I've worked on this, and have come to the realization that this person treats everyone badly, and that's not likely to change.

By releasing that expectation, I've been able to focus on accepting the person for who they are, without the disappointment in how they behave. This has resulted in fewer hurt feelings for me!

I think the overall lesson here is: don't settle for things that aren't quite right or have served their purpose in your life.

When we hang on to the past, we cannot move into the future. Even Tarzan had to let go of the vine behind him in order to move forward!

The guy who isn't The One, or the friend who makes you feel bad about yourself, or the toaster oven that doesn't toast are not making your life One-Derful.

What makes life One-Derful is knowing that you are okay and you are able to have a better life when you let go of the broken things (relationships, appliances, people) and make room for the things you really want.

And, feel free to call me if you need pens, notepads, or refrigerator magnets!

Give It Up

I am knee-deep in spring cleaning! Out with the old, in with the new!

As it turns out, I may be just a few items away from being classified as a hoarder. I've learned some interesting things about myself: I can stop stealing pens from hotels and banks; I have 87 pencils even though I never use pencils; I have the world's largest collection of clothes hangers.

As I have been rooting through my possessions, I have found a lot of items that were taking up space for no good reason. For example, the adding machine tape rolls to the adding machine that broke 5 years ago. I threw away the machine, but kept the tapes.

Or, there is every magazine I ever subscribed to (no kidding).

And, one of my favorites: medication bottles from my dog's prescriptions from 10 years ago.

As I've been sorting, donating, and tossing, I have created something I've never had in my home: empty drawers and shelves.

It's odd – those empty spaces devoid of clutter, but it's nice. And, I've made room for some things that I really did need (like a pencil sharpener), as well as room for nicer things (hello, upgraded desk accessories!).

All this tossing and replacing reflects some other experiences I'm having in my life.

I'm learning that in order to have some new experiences in my life, I may have to give up some things.

If I want to "get over it," I have to give up thinking about "it" all the time (whatever the "it" drama is).

If I want to have peace in my life, I have to trust God.

If I want to have good relationships with people, I have to change how I interact.

I recently had a conversation with a friend of mine where he said something that normally would send me into an emotional tornado of hurt and insecurity. I started to react with my normal tools: shutting down and running away; but then I remembered that I want to do things differently in my relationships. So, I asked some questions about what he was saying and then tried to relate to where he was.

I was still anxious, but I was able to communicate from a place of compassion. My friend was struggling with a difficult situation; I was able to reflect on a similar time in my life, and was able to offer the understanding that I wanted when I was struggling.

The result: my friend felt accepted by me, and it made our friendship stronger. That is major growth for me, people!

In Isaiah, God says He will give us "beauty for ashes, the oil of gladness for mourning, and a garment of praise instead of a spirit of despair" (see Isaiah 61:3).

We all want the beauty, the gladness, and the lightness of praise. But here's the catch: we have to give up the ashes of our past, our mourning (pouting, self-pity), and our despair (moping and negativity). We cannot keep our resentments and selfish behaviors and also receive the blessings.

I cannot have space in my house and also keep all of the stuff. I cannot have space in my life and keep all the activities. I cannot have space in my heart and keep all the pain.

I had to ask myself, "Why do I keep all this stuff?" My answer: "in case I need it later." That is fear talking. Translation: "What if I need this later and I don't have it? I won't be okay."

The Lord showed me recently that there are certain areas where I want to fail. That sounds ridiculous, but if you have repeatedly failed at something, you know how to handle the hurt, disappointment, and self-doubt. I know to go to God, pray, and let Him soothe my pain. That's not scary to me: I know how to walk the road of emotional recovery.

What scares me is success in love. I've never experienced success in the area of relationships, so I don't know what to do. That road requires me to lean on God for every single step because I have no idea where that road leads. To succeed, I have to trust God. I have to let go of my roadmap and let Him lead me.

There's not room on the narrow path for all of our stuff and emotional clutter. The One-Derful Life requires that we jettison some of our emotional baggage. The Lord told me to get rid of some of my fear; if I need it later, there is an ample supply for me to draw from!

How to Celebrate Your Singleness

In my younger days I could think of no worse fate than to be single in my 40's. Today, I am well over 40 and still single, and I am living a One-derful Life. Here are some reasons to celebrate if you're single and over 40.

You have a life. One of the best things about being single in over 40 is that you have a full life. You have a career (how else are you paying your bills?), you have interests, you have friends, and you have fun things to do. This well-rounded life makes you attractive.

Even if you don't meet someone (or don't want to meet someone) to date, you have an interesting life and you're not waiting on someone to entertain you.

I recently had a date with a gentleman who was complaining that he was bored and didn't have anything to do because he didn't have a girlfriend "to do stuff with."

That was simultaneously our last date, as my takeaway from that conversation was that I would have to entertain him. And, since he was bored, he was also boring. Don't have a life? Get one!

You have standards. When you're single in your 20's, you're more likely to put up with bad behavior from people you date because you don't know any better.

In your 30's you may feel desperate, so you put up with bad behavior because you think it's better than being alone.

By your 40's, you know that being alone is way better than being with someone who treats you badly, because at least if you're alone, nobody is being mean to you.

You're not afraid of being "left" because you're comfortable being by yourself.

The fact that you are secure on your own makes you attractive because you're not coming across as desperate or needy.

You know what you want. By this point, you know what you want out of a relationship. Either you want to get married and have children (soon!), or you want to get married (no children, please), or you want a committed relationship, or you just want to have fun.

You know what kind of people you're attracted to, and you know what is important to you and what makes you compatible with someone you're dating.

You know what you don't want. More importantly, you know what you don't want in a partner.

Personally, I don't date men with criminal records, wives, bankruptcies, or who are currently unemployed. Nor do I date men who are substance abusers, who don't share my faith, or who are really big jerks.

Knowing what you DON'T want will help you not waste your time and energy on dates which will leave you feeling frustrated and depressed.

You have learned to accept yourself. In my 20's and 30's, if a man didn't like me, I figured I was too fat or not pretty enough or not blonde enough.

In my 40's I have accepted and made peace with my figure flaws. I know I can fluctuate by 5-7 pounds from my current weight, but if I need to lose 10 pounds to catch your eye, I'm not the girl for you. And I don't get upset about it anymore.

It turns out that men consistently rate "confidence" as one of a woman's sexiest traits. So do the best you can with what you have. You're not going to be able to compete with women in their 20's, so don't waste your time trying. Just be the best 40-year old YOU that you can be.

You are able to speak for yourself. In your 40's, you have the confidence to express your feelings, thoughts, wants, and needs. You also should have the ability to listen and answer others. This saves you countless hours of anxiety because you can just talk about whatever the problem is.

You won't find yourself eating at restaurants you hate, participating in activities you cannot stand, or going to parties with people you dislike.

If you're still going along silently with these things (other than the holidays, which are all about people, food, and events you may dislike) in your forties, then shame on you! Find your voice, use your words, and speak up!

Being single in your 40's is a One-Derful adventure. By now you may have some money, so you can travel and build the life you want to have. Don't wait to be a wife to have a life!

While you're enjoying your life, you will be attractive to those around you and you may end up meeting an interesting gentleman friend. If not, you'll just continue to enjoy yourself!

Thoughts & Thanks

For years, people told me I "should write a book." Well, here it is!

Thank you to my mother, Catherine, and my father, Henry. You raised me to be hard-working, self-reliant, and resilient. You have always supported and encouraged me. I love you very much.

To my brother, Henry, and my sister-in-law, Sarah - thank you for all of the encouragement, support, and love over the years. You have been two of my most powerful teachers.

To Hannah and Beau, Aunt Mayna loves you both very much!

To the first author I ever knew, my uncle, Dr. Ralph E. Dittman - I remember indexing your book BY HAND, and loving every minute of it!

To my grandparents, Mary and Mitch Cobeaga, and Ruth and Henry Dittman - I love you and miss you.

To my uncle, Mitch Cobeaga - I miss you and I love you.

To my stepmother, Sandra, I miss you, as well. Thank you for showing me how to be a stepmother. I hope someday I will be able to put into practice what you taught me.

To my truest girlfriends who have stood by me throughout the good times and the not-so-good: Erinne O'Hara Aboytes, Elizabeth Zahnd Bergfeld, Melissa Bickers Bone, Susanne Owens,

Kay Wall Woodberry, and Nancy Zaice. I love you all so much!

To Dr. Fred Carter, Dr. Richard Chapman, Dr. Peter King, Dr. Barry O'Brien, and Dr. Hari Rajagopalan - thank you for teaching me how to teach and for giving me the opportunity to serve all these years.

To Melia Flowers, my first editor. Thank you for teaching me how to express myself in writing.

To my coaches, Valentina Galante and Kelly Mishell - thank you for holding me up when I was weak and for celebrating with me when I was victorious!

To my mentors, most of whom I have not yet met - thank you for your guidance and wisdom. Brendon Burchard, Deepak Chopra, Marie Forleo, Charlene Johnson, Iyanla Vanzant, and Marianne Williamson - I am grateful for your teachings that have helped me all these years.

Thank you to the One-Derful Life tribe - I love you all!

About The Author

Mary R. Dittman, M.B.A. is an award-winning professor, writer, and speaker. She is the creator of College On Fleek and One-Derful Life.

Learn more at One-DerfulLife.com.

Made in the USA
Columbia, SC
17 August 2019